TEXAS
WRITE
SOURCE

SkillsBook

Grade 5

GREAT
SOURCE®

HOUGHTON MIFFLIN HARCOURT

A Few Words About the
Texas Write Source SkillsBook Grade 5

Before you begin . . .

The *SkillsBook* provides you with opportunities to practice editing and proofreading skills presented in the Student Edition of *Texas Write Source*. That book contains guidelines, examples, and models to help you complete your work in the *SkillsBook*.

Each *SkillsBook* activity includes instruction on the topic and examples showing how to complete that activity. You will be directed to the page numbers in the Student Edition of *Texas Write Source* for additional information and examples. The "Proofreading Activities" focus on the mechanics of writing (including punctuation), spelling, and usage. The "Sentence Activities" provide practice in sentence combining and in correcting common sentence problems. The "Language Activities" highlight the parts of speech.

Most activities end with **The Next Step** or **Learning Language** to help you apply what you have learned to your own writing.

Photo Acknowledgements Cover ©Corbis; 85 ©Digital Vision/Getty Images; 135 ©Alaskan Express/Jupiter Images.

Copyright © by Houghton Mifflin Harcourt Publishing Company

Printed in the U.S.A.

ISBN-13   978-0-547-39563-0

8 9 10 0982 19 18 17 16 15 14 13

4500414276   BCDEFG

Table of Contents
Proofreading Activities

Sentence Activities

Sentence Basics

Sentence Problems

Sentence Variety

Language Activities

Nouns

Pronouns

Verbs

Adjectives

Editing for Mechanics

Every activity in this section includes sentences that need to be checked for punctuation, grammar, sentence structure, capitalization, or spelling. Most of the activities also include helpful references to the Student Edition of *Texas Write Source*. In addition, **The Next Step** and **Learning Language**, which are at the end of most activities, encourage follow-up practice of certain skills.

ELPS 2C, 4C

End Punctuation 1

Using the correct **end punctuation** is a basic step in punctuating your writing. There are three kinds of end punctuation: the period, the question mark, and the exclamation point. (See *Texas Write Source* pages 523 and 524.)

Examples

Native Americans welcomed the Pilgrims.

When was that?

That was back in 1620!

Directions ▶ Put the correct end punctuation—a period, a question mark, or an exclamation point—in the sentences below. Capitalize the first letter of each sentence. The first sentence has been done for you.

1   Have you ever wondered who the very first Americans were?

2   scientists say they came from Asia thousands of years ago at that

3   time, land connected Asia to the part of North America that is now

4   Alaska. imagine that people followed herds of animals across the

5   "land bridge" between Asia and America these people needed to use

6   the animals for food and clothing it was much too cold to grow crops

7   the first Americans slowly moved farther and farther south

8   after thousands of years, their ancestors reached the tip of South

9   America wow that's a lot of walking!

The Next Step Write a paragraph describing your coldest experience. In at least two places, try to use a word, a phrase, or a sentence that would require an exclamation point.

ELPS 4C

Directions   In the following sentences, add commas between items in a series. The first sentence has been done for you.

1. All Olympic runners practice every day, drink lots of fluids, and carefully, pace themselves.

2. Some famous women runners are Mary Decker, Gwen Torrence, and Florence Griffith-Joyner.

3. These runners have won titles in national, world, and Olympic races.

4. All of these women have worked hard, overcome injuries, and won titles.

5. One was a champion, in sprinting one was a winner in middle distance, and one was a long-distance title holder.

6. Have you heard about Joan Benoit Samuelson, who had a dream, pushed toward, it and never gave up?

7. She ran in high school, in college, and in the 1979, Boston Marathon.

8. Joan was an unknown, a clear winner, and a record breaker.

9. She also won the 1983 Boston Marathon, the 1984 U.S. Olympic time trials, and the 1984 Olympic Marathon.

10. Three miles into the Olympic race, Benoit Samuelson, moved ahead, kept the lead, and won easily.

11. Joan Benoit Samuelson, is a role model, an author, and an Olympic gold medal winner.

Commas in Compound Sentences

A **comma** may be used with a coordinating conjunction to join two independent clauses. Coordinating conjunctions are words such as *and, but,* or *so.* (See *Texas Write Source* 526.3.)

Example

Comma and Coordinating Conjunction:
I know the words to "The Star-Spangled Banner," **but** I can't hit all the notes!

(*Note:* The comma is placed inside the quotation marks.)

 **Directions** In the paragraph below, add commas between independent clauses joined by coordinating conjunctions. The first sentence has been done for you.

1   Americans have been singing "The Star-Spangled Banner"

2   since the early 1800s, but it didn't become the official national

3   anthem until 1931. On November 3, 1929, newspapers announced

4   that there was no official anthem so people began to think about

5   a national song. More than 5 million people wrote to ask Congress

6   to choose one but many of these people didn't want "The Star-

7   Spangled Banner." Some people were bothered by two things: the

8   music was written in England and the United States had fought

9   against England for freedom in 1776. "America" and a few other

10   songs received votes but "The Star-Spangled Banner" won the day.

ELPS 4C

11. All insects have six legs don't they?

12. Hey that's right!

13. Look here the butterflies on page 244 have only four legs.

14. You are right hmm.

15. Wait there are front legs held against the butterfly's body.

16. Oh now I see the tiny front legs.

The Next Step Write a paragraph about fish, birds, or snakes. Use some interjections and interruptions in several of the sentences. Be sure you properly set off the interjections and interruptions with commas.

_____

_____

_____

_____

_____

_____

_____

_____

ELPS 2C, 4C

Commas to Separate Equal Adjectives

If two or more adjectives equally modify a noun, separate them with a **comma**. How can you tell if the adjectives are equal? Reverse the order of the adjectives. If the meaning of the sentence does not change, the adjectives are equal.

Examples

Two Adjectives That Modify a Noun Equally:
Jen thought the **cool, clear** water tasted good.
(Jen thought the **clear, cool** water tasted good.)

Two Adjectives That Do Not Modify the Noun Equally:
Evans picked up the **silver wedding** ring.
(Evans picked up the **wedding silver** ring.)

 **Directions** ▶ In the following paragraph, put commas between equal adjectives. The first one has been done. (See *Texas Write Source* 532.1 for more information.)

1   Because Rafer liked doing tricks, he needed a strong, sturdy

2   scooter. He really liked the new popular Laser J55 model, but it

3   cost almost $60. One day he saw an ad on the school bulletin

4   board for a four-year-old Jet B37 scooter for $10. This would be a

5   cheap dependable scooter until he could get a Laser. The scooter

6   had faded streaked paint on the deck. He could tell the deck had

7   a thin sharp edge on one side, but his dad could fix that. Rafer

8   liked the looks of the chrome wheelie bar, but he didn't like the

9   thick hard wheels. After he used the scooter, he decided he really

10   liked it.

ELPS 2C, 4C

Commas to Set Off Appositives

Commas are used in many different ways. Commas set off **appositives**. An appositive is a word or phrase that *renames* or *explains* a noun that comes before the word or phrase. (See *Texas Write Source* 532.2.)

Example

Cooper Elementary**, my school,** has 250 students.

Directions ▶ **Use commas to set off the appositives in the following paragraph. The first sentence has been done for you.**

1   Mrs. Chang, our teacher, won an award. The award a gift

2   certificate was for being an excellent teacher. Our principal Mrs.

3   Greene presented the award. Mrs. Chang the best teacher I've had

4   yet deserved to win. Alisha a girl in our class read a poem about

5   Mrs. Chang. Mrs. Chang's husband a math teacher was there. The

6   rest of us sang a song "You're the Best" for Mrs. Chang. Bobby

7   a talented composer wrote the song. We all wrote stories favorite

8   classroom memories to put in a booklet for our great teacher.

9   Tamara a computer whiz made a banner on her computer. The

10   banner a work of art said, "Way to go, Mrs. Chang!"

The Next Step Write four sentences, each one saying something about a different person you know. Start each sentence with the person's name, add an appositive that tells something about the person, and then finish the sentence.

ELPS 2C, 4C

Commas to Set Off Explanatory Phrases

Commas are used to set off **explanatory phrases** from the rest of the sentence. Explanatory phrases add information. (See *Texas Write Source* 532.2.)

Example

SpaceShipOne, **funded by a private company**, set an altitude record.

Directions ▶ Use commas to set off the explanatory phrases in the following sentences.

1. Mike Melvill the first commercial astronaut to pilot *SpaceShipOne* flew the craft at more than 1,800 miles per hour.

2. A jet called the *White Knight* built by a company called Scaled Composites carried the spacecraft to 50,000 feet.

3. On October 4, 2004, Brian Binnie the second pilot to fly *SpaceShipOne* felt the powerful rocket climb into space.

4. Then the rocket its engines shut off reached a record 69.6 miles.

5. Melvill's and Binnie's flights completed within a week of each other meant Scaled Composites won a $10 million prize.

6. A special group made up of people wanting to promote space travel first offered the Ansari X Prize back in May 1996.

7. Richard Branson hoping to take paying travelers into space announced his new company would charge $200,000 per ride.

TEKS 5.21B(i)
ELPS 4C

Comma Review 1

This activity is a review of the different ways in which you've learned to use commas. (Review *Texas Write Source* pages 526–533.)

Directions ▶ **Add commas where they are needed in the following paragraph.**

1 If you sometimes feel like sleeping all winter you might in

2 fact like to have a groundhog's life. Groundhogs also known as

3 woodchucks sleep for six months every year. Wow that's a long

4 winter's nap. Although Groundhog Day is February 2 groundhogs

5 rarely wake up before April! While a groundhog hibernates its

6 body temperature drops, and its heart rate slows down.

7 Bears raccoons and skunks which at least wake up for midwinter

8 snacks don't sleep as deeply as groundhogs. Insects reptiles and

9 amphibians also hibernate but they don't sleep as deeply as

10 groundhogs either. Insects hide under tree bark beneath logs and

11 in leaf litter. Amphibians which can easily dry out burrow into

12 mud to escape the cold. While turtles often dig into the mud as

13 well snakes find caves old wells or wood piles for the long winter.

14 In fact groundhogs some of the deepest sleeping of all hibernating

15 creatures are rarely seen in winter and now you know why.

 TEKS 5.21B(i)
ELPS 4C

Comma Review 2

This activity is a review of the different ways in which you've learned to use commas. (Review *Texas Write Source* pages 526–533.)

Directions ▶ Add commas to correctly punctuate the following sentences.

1. On July 20 1969 Neil Armstrong was the first person to walk on the moon.

2. Sally Ride an astronaut flew into space in 1983.

3. Lewis and Clark's famous historic journey began on May 14 1804 and ended on September 23 1806.

4. The Apollo program planned for moon exploration began in 1963.

5. Lincoln delivered his Gettysburg Address on November 19 1863.

6. In the Civil War General Robert E. Lee surrendered on April 9 1865 and the last Southern soldiers surrendered on May 26 1865.

7. Parking for Independence Hall is at 1518 Walnut Street Philadelphia Pennsylvania.

8. The largest most powerful rocket ever built was the *Saturn V.*

9. Hawaii became the 50th state on August 21 1959.

10. The White House is located at 1600 West Pennsylvania Avenue NW Washington D.C.

TEKS 5.21B(i)
ELPS 4C

Commas and End Punctuation Review

This activity is a review of commas and end punctuation. (See *Texas Write Source* pages 523–533.)

Directions ▶ Add needed commas and end punctuation marks in the sentences below. Also capitalize the first letter of each new sentence. The first sentence has been done for you.

1   In the early 1800's, only about half of the children in the

2   United States went to school. at that time, many people thought

3   that only boys should go to school so girls were usually not allowed

4   to attend

5   However, Sara Pierce started a school for girls and she taught

6   the girls grammar reading writing and history one of her students

7   was Harriet Beecher Stowe ms. Stowe later wrote a famous novel

8   called *Uncle Tom's Cabin* Mary Lyon founded the first college to

9   accept women and that college was called Mount Holyoke College

10   Emily Dickinson another great writer was a student there

11   one teacher became famous for writing books for both boys

12   and girls he wrote the first American dictionary and his name is

13   still on many dictionaries can you guess his name sure you can

14   his name is Noah Webster

⭐ ELPS 2C, 4C

Apostrophes 1

Apostrophes can be used to make contractions. (See *Texas Write Source* 534.1.)

Examples

you + will = **you'll**   I + am = **I'm**

have + not = **haven't**   would + not = **wouldn't**

Directions ▶ In the following paragraph, use apostrophes to make as many contractions as you can. The first one has been done for you.

1   *doesn't*
    Jessica ~~does not~~ like to sit in class on warm spring days.

2   She would rather be out playing baseball with Juan and Jennifer.

3   They are all baseball nuts. They will spend all summer playing

4   baseball, I am sure. Jessica always says it is too nice to be inside, even

5   if it is raining. I like baseball, too, but I do not like to play in the rain.

6   On rainy days, I would rather play computer games, but that does not

7   last. Those games can not hold my attention for long. The sound of the

8   rain on the window makes me want to sleep. I know I should not take

9   a nap in the afternoon, but I can not keep my eyes open. Suddenly, I will

10   awaken and discover it is supper time. That means I will not be able

11   to go to my best friend's house. I will have to stay up late to finish my

12   homework. Maybe I should not play computer games on a rainy day.

The Next Step Write a sentence for each of the following word groups using the contraction form: *I am, you are, could not, it will,* and *they would.*

ELPS 2C, 4C

Apostrophes 2

Apostrophes are sometimes used to show possession. (See 534.2 and 536.1.)

Examples

Singular Possession: The **nurse's** stethoscope was missing.

Plural Possession: The **nurses'** station had three nurses.

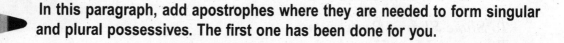

Directions ▶ In this paragraph, add apostrophes where they are needed to form singular and plural possessives. The first one has been done for you.

1   Peoples dreams of future careers often involve helping those in

2   need. From the age of 11, Clara Bartons goal was to be a nurse. A

3   brothers illness showed her that she liked to help sick people. Later,

4   with her fathers permission, she went to help soldiers in the Civil War.

5   Clara found out there weren't enough bandages for soldiers wounds.

6   She decided to do something. With some senators support, Clara was

7   able to bring much needed medical supplies to the battlefield. Often

8   she stood by doctors sides as bullets whizzed by. Several years after the

9   war, she traveled to Europe to help the wounded and suffering during

10   the Franco-Prussian War. Because she was so impressed with the

11   International Red Crosss work, she later founded Americas Red Cross

12   in 1881. Clara traveled many times to help several countries starving

13   people. Clara Barton will always be remembered for her unselfish

14   devotion to the worlds people.

ELPS 2C, 4C

Apostrophes 3

Apostrophes are sometimes used to show some plurals and shared possession. (To get ready, review *Texas Write Source* 536.3 and 536.4.)

Examples

To Form Some Plurals:
It is an invention with **+ 's** and **– 's**.

To Show Shared Possession:
Tom and **Marci's** calculator is powered by sunlight.

Directions ▶ **Add apostrophes where they are needed in the following sentences.**

1. Young students need to learn their A, B, Cs.

2. Fern, Bill, and Jacks science project is due this week.

3. How many 5828s are there in the national phone system?

4. That paragraph has too many "becauses" in it.

5. I was told to pick up John and Michelles homework.

6. Why are there so many +s in this math problem?

7. This award is Jane, Tony, Saul, and Jakes.

8. Antoine's report card had two As, four Bs, and no Cs.

9. The boys and girls playground has new equipment.

10. As Phil checked his story, he saw he had too many "awesomes" in it.

ELPS 4C

Apostrophes Review

Directions **Add all the apostrophes needed in the following sentences. Form plurals, contractions, and possessive nouns using apostrophes.**

1. An oil tankers anchor weighs hundreds of pounds.

2. Big ships can not stop quickly.

3. Arlene, Rafe, and Sues cruise ship leaves for the Caribbean tomorrow.

4. Boys clothes are in aisle 15 next to boots and shoes.

5. Football coaches like to use Xs and Os when drawing plays on the

   blackboard.

6. I think you will like the color of your new bike.

7. Do not forget to bring your notebooks to class on Thursday.

8. Jared likes to draw 9s and 15s all over the cover of his notebook.

9. Sharks, bears, and wolves jaws are very strong.

10. Tom said he would rather paint a fence than do nothing all day.

11. He knew his paper needed reworking when he saw all the !s and *s.

12. Place the girls team jerseys on the table.

TEKS 5.21B(ii)
ELPS 2C, 4C

Quotation Marks 1

What do **quotation marks** mark? In dialogue, they mark the exact words a person speaks. They are also used to mark the titles of songs, poems, short stories, articles, and so on. (See *Texas Write Source* page 538.)

Example

"Hi," Angelo said. "Where are you going?"

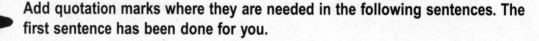

Directions Add quotation marks where they are needed in the following sentences. The first sentence has been done for you.

1. Ricardo said, "I'm going to the library. Do you want to come?"

2. No, I answered. But will you check out a book for me?

3. Sure, Ricardo said. What book do you want?

4. I asked for any book that included nature poems like the poem Birdfoot's Grampa or the poem Something Told the Wild Geese.

5. Here are some great poems by Joseph Bruchac, Ricardo said.

6. I told him I hadn't read any of Joseph Bruchac's poems yet, but I saw one called The Song of Small Things in my literature book.

7. Be sure to read it, Ric said. It's awesome!

8. I will, I said. If all the poems are about nature, I'll like them!

The Next Step Write down a conversation you and a friend have had about school, sports, books, or movies. Be sure to use quotation marks correctly.

TEKS 5.21B(ii)
ELPS 2C, 4C

Quotation Marks 2

Quotation marks are used to set off dialogue. Place quotation marks before and after the spoken words. A new paragraph should begin every time the speaker changes.

Example "Soccer is my favorite sport," Maria said.

 **Directions** **Rewrite the dialogue below. Add quotation marks where they are needed. Also start a new paragraph each time a different person speaks.**

Did you see the game yesterday? Rodrigo shouted as he jogged up the steps leading to the art room. Yeah, it was great! Maria shouted back. I didn't think we had a chance. I mean, two goals to zero with only two minutes—I know! Rodrigo interrupted. I switched the channel twice before I realized what was happening. What a rally! Now it's the semifinals against Brazil, whispered Maria as they headed for their seats in the front row.

_____

_____

_____

_____

_____

_____

_____

_____

_____

 TEKS 5.21B(ii)
ELPS 2C, 4C

Quotation Marks 3

Use **quotation marks** to set off a person's exact words in a story. The quotation marks should enclose the spoken words. Remember to begin a new paragraph with each new speaker.

Example "Let's go skating this afternoon," said Anne.

Directions Rewrite the dialogue below. Add quotation marks where they are needed. Remember to begin a new paragraph with each new speaker.

Welcome! said Katie as she greeted her friends. I'm so glad you could come to my party. Well, you said it was going to be a different kind of party, Carlos responded. I was certainly curious. You know what they say, chimed in Lucy. Curiosity killed the cat! So what is the big surprise? asked Carlos. Well, instead of my planning the party, we all will, Katie beamed. That's why I asked you to each bring a board game.

_____

_____

_____

_____

_____

_____

_____

TEKS 5.21B(ii)
ELPS 2C, 4C

Punctuating Dialogue

Written dialogue follows definite rules. Place quotation marks before and after the spoken words. Put periods and commas *inside* quotation marks. Place question marks and exclamation points *inside* the quotation marks when they punctuate the quotation; *outside* when they punctuate the main sentence. Direct quotations begin with capital letters.

Example

"Hey, Craig!" yelled Bill. "Wait for me!"

Directions ▸ **Write in any missing punctuation in the following dialogue. Also correct any errors in capitalization.**

1   Hi, Bill I said. Did you buy any new baseball cards at the

2   store

3   Yes, I did Bill answered with a smile. I had enough money

4   to buy 10 packs.

5   Great did you open the packs yet

6   No do you want to help me?

7   Sure! I hope you get some doubles I said. I will buy them

8   from you.

9   Maybe we could trade Bill answered.

10   Let's open the packs and see what you got first

 **TEKS** 5.21B(ii)
ELPS 4C

Punctuating Dialogue Review

Directions ▶ In the following dialogue sentences, add the correct end punctuation, quotation marks, and capitalization.

1 Wait a minute Jorge said Sonja wants you to take her article to

2 the newspaper

3 Sanchez said what article

4 Jorge answered it's her article about our field trip last week to the

5 mint

6 Oh, that one said Sanchez am I in the story

7 Yes, you are

8 I want to see what she wrote! exclaimed Sanchez It was fun.

9 Sonja wrote about all of us and the trip, but she singles you out

10 for praise responded Jorge.

11 Why did she do that Sanchez asked

12 you helped Terry get around in his wheelchair, Jorge said.

13 I didn't mind doing that, said Sanchez. My sister has to use

14 crutches, so I am used to helping.

15 Well, whether you are used to it or not, replied Jorge, Sonja was

16 impressed with your kindness.

ELPS 2C, 4C

Hyphens

Hyphens are explained on *Texas Write Source* page 540. The following activities give you practice using hyphens.

Examples

With Compound Adjectives:
My sister chews **sugar-free** gum.

Between Syllables:
She also likes to eat frozen orange juice **con-centrate** right from the can.

With Compound Words:
The **president-elect** waits more than two months to take office.

 **Put hyphens where they are needed in the sentences below. The first sentence has been done for you.**

1. Mom puts big pieces of chocolate in her chocolate‑chunk cookies.

2. The governor elect has a lot to learn about her new job.

3. My great grandfather was a well known doctor.

4. I once made a long distance call to Japan.

5. I have an eight year old cousin who looks like me.

6. Dad's sister in law took a well deserved vacation.

7. Jon is an all purpose running back for our team.

8. My friend Sam likes well done hamburgers.

9. They covered the roof with blue green tiles.

ELPS 4C

Directions ▶ Use hyphens to show how you could divide the following words at the end of a line. (Some words should not be divided.)

1. history ___his-to-ry___   6. contents _____

2. writing _____   7. connection _____

3. item _____   8. microscope _____

4. revise _____   9. anyone _____

5. improving _____   10. doesn't _____

Directions ▶ Using the compound words listed below, fill in the blanks to complete the story.

well-timed   fun-filled   well-known   old-fashioned
well-equipped   far-distant   sun-warmed

1   Most of the class had never seen a lake as big as Lake

2   Erie. Some thought the _____ lake looked like the ocean.

3   Because Lake Erie is so wide, the students could not see the

4   _____ shore. Before going on their _____ trip,

5   they found out that four states and one province border Lake Erie.

6   The students also learned that _____ boats catch more

7   fish in Erie than the other four Great Lakes combined. The reason

8   is that the _____ lake is so shallow that fish seem to do

9   well. The class had fun learning about Lake Erie, seeing the lake,

10   and riding on an _____ tour boat. Still, everyone agreed

11   that a _____ swim was a good way to end the day.

★ ELPS 2C, 4C

Colons 1

A **colon** can be used to introduce a list in a sentence and to express time. (See *Texas Write Source* page 542.)

Examples

I am interested in the following mammals: whales, dolphins, and porpoises.

Our field trip departed for the zoo at 8:30 a.m. on Tuesday.

Directions ▶ Add colons to introduce the lists in the sentences below. Also add colons to express time. The first sentence has been done for you.

1. Reptiles have the following things in common: they have backbones, most hatch their young from eggs, and they are cold-blooded.

2. The following are all reptiles turtles, alligators, and crocodiles.

3. Alligators and crocodiles have some things in common they have webbed feet, their eyes and nostrils are high on their heads, and they are able to open their mouths underwater without drowning.

4. There are two ways to identify alligators by their rounded snouts and by their upper teeth, which are seen even when their mouths are closed!

5. Here are the telltale signs of a crocodile a pointed snout and two lower teeth sticking out when its mouth is closed.

⭐ ELPS 4C

6. The following are all amphibians salamanders, frogs, and toads.

7. In the Everglades, you can see alligators at the Gulf Coast Visitor Center from 900 a.m. to 430 p.m. all summer.

8. Outside the park, airboat tours run from 800 a.m. to 500 p.m.

Directions ▶ In the paragraph below, add colons to introduce the lists and to express time.

1   Florida is home to three interesting lizards geckos, glass

2   lizards, and iguanids. Lizards are very similar to snakes; however,

3   unlike snakes, most lizards have three features legs, external ear

4   openings, and eyelids. Geckos are most active in the early evening

5   from 500 to 700. They can do two interesting things they can

6   quickly shed their tails (which regenerate), and they can walk

7   upside down across ceilings. Glass lizards are known as "glass

8   snakes" for two reasons their long tails break off very easily, and

9   they have no legs. These lizards enjoy certain "bugs" for dinner

10 crickets, grasshoppers, and spiders. Iguanids are the lizards often

11 called "chameleons." Besides changing color to blend with their

12 surroundings, these lizards seem to enjoy three activities head

13 bobbing, head nodding, and push-ups.

The Next Step Write a sentence of your own about a favorite animal. Include a colon to introduce a list.

⬟ **ELPS** 2C, 4C

Colons 2

Another way a **colon** is used is to make a formal introduction of a quotation. (See *Texas Write Source* 542.2.)

Example

Joan Lowery Nixon said this about writing:
"The idea is just the beginning of the story."

Directions ▶ Add colons where they are needed in the following sentences.

1. On the subject of honesty, Mark Twain said this "Truth is stranger than fiction—to some people."

2. I thought of something Abraham Lincoln said "It's a good rule never to send a mouse to catch a skunk, or a polliwog to tackle a whale."

3. I was scared, and I remembered this line from *The Lion, the Witch, and the Wardrobe* "Peter did not feel very brave; indeed, he felt he was going to be sick."

4. In *The Adventures of Sherlock Holmes*, Holmes says this about life "My dear fellow, life is infinitely stranger than anything the mind of man could invent."

ELPS 4C

5. Ben Franklin wrote in his *Poor Richard's Almanac* "Well done is better than well said."

6. When interviewed about his space flight, Russian cosmonaut Yuri Gagarin excitedly said "I could have gone on flying through space forever."

The Next Step Now write three sentences of your own in which you use colons to introduce quotations. (Look them up in a book of quotations, or take them from a favorite book.)

1. _____

_____

_____

2. _____

_____

_____

3. _____

_____

_____

⭐ **ELPS** 2C, 4C

Semicolons

Semicolons tell the reader to pause, or even stop, before reading the rest of the sentence. (See *Texas Write Source* page 544.)

Examples

To Join Two Independent Clauses:
I have a cat; he's a blur of gray fur.

To Separate Groups in a Series with Commas:
I need to buy cat food, cat toys, and litter; clean the cat box, hallway, and closet; and give Fuzzball a brushing.

▶ **Directions**   Each sentence below contains two independent clauses that are separated by a comma and a conjunction. Replace the comma and conjunction with a semicolon. The first sentence has been done for you.

1   Roy C. Sullivan was a park ranger, yet his life was more

2   exciting than you might think. He was struck by lightning seven

3   times, but he lived to tell about it. No one understood why

4   Sullivan kept getting hit by lightning, and it's amazing that he

5   kept working! Lightning "fried" several of his hats, and one time

6   it set fire to his hair.

The Next Step Write a sentence using the set of phrases below. Be sure to use semicolons appropriately in your new sentence.

see the lions, tigers, and bears ■ eat hot dogs, ice cream, and cotton

candy ■ run home in time for supper

Italics and Underlining 1

Italics are explained on *Texas Write Source* page 546. In many publications, titles of books are shown in italics. However you may **underline** book, newspaper, magazine, and movie titles in your writing.

Example

Louisa May Alcott wrote <u>Little Women</u>, a book about her family.

Directions ▶ In the following sentences, underline all titles that should be in italics.

1. Washington Irving wrote a book of stories called The Sketch Book. Rip Van Winkle, who slept for 20 years, is a character in it.

2. Phillis Wheatley was a slave who was brought to America when she was about seven. She never went to school, but she wrote poetry that was published in London Magazine.

3. James Fenimore Cooper wrote about the sea and pioneer life. He wrote successful novels like The Last of the Mohicans, The Prairie, and The Deerslayer.

4. Early American writers created tall tales about larger-than-life heroes. Modern writer Steven Kellogg also wrote tall tales and made two of them into books called Paul Bunyan and Pecos Bill.

TEKS 5.21C
ELPS 2C, 4C

Italics and Underlining 2

Italics can also be used to emphasize a word or phrase. Do not overuse italics for emphasis, as they will lose their effect. To show emphasis in your handwriting, you may **underline.**

Examples

Monica thinks *she* has the best science project.

I can't believe my cousin is getting *another* dog.

In each sentence below, underline a word or phrase that should be italicized to show emphasis.

1. "Our team is in last place. But yesterday something amazing happened. We won the game!" Rueben exclaimed.

2. Christina is such a good student, so you can imagine how upset she was when her little brother decided to shred her English composition for fun.

3. Mr. Ross paid Garrett twenty dollars just to water his plants while he was on vacation!

4. Ms. Jackson said she wanted us to read the book by next Friday.

5. Have you heard the news? Our school is getting a brand new auditorium, complete with surround-sound speakers!

TEKS 5.21C
ELPS 4C

Italics and Underlining 3

Remember, if you want to emphasize words or phrases, you may use **italics** or **underlining.** If you use a computer, use italics to show emphasis. In handwritten material, underline the words.

Examples

The spilled cranberry juice *ruined* my grandmother's lace tablecloth.

Rick's painting was chosen over <u>twenty-two</u> other contestants!

 **Directions** **In each sentence below, underline a word or phrase that should be italicized to show emphasis.**

1. After Staci dove into the river, she surfaced and shouted, "This water is cold!"

2. Six-year-old Hunter painted a mural on his wall with permanent ink. Although he thought it was a good idea, his mother did not.

3. Are you going to Belle's party or mine?

4. The recipe calls for three eggs, not four.

5. Shawna's dog, Roger, chased after the delivery truck, then jumped right in and sat next to the driver.

6. When Mrs. Wolcott heard there would be very important people at the party, she had no idea the queen would be there.

TEKS 5.21C
ELPS 4C

Italics and Quotation Marks

To punctuate titles in your writing, the general rule is that titles of complete works (such as books) are italicized or underlined. Titles of parts of works (such as chapters) are put in quotation marks.

Texas Write Source 538.3 explains which titles need quotation marks, and 546.1 explains which titles should be italicized or underlined.

Examples

My favorite chapter in <u>Texas Write Source</u> is "Writing Poems."

"Too Many Cats!" is a story in a book called <u>Cat Tales</u>.

 **In the following sentences, put quotation marks around the titles that need them, and underline titles that should be in italic type.**

1. The Lion King and Aladdin are movies with great songs.

2. Our science book has chapters called The Planets and Beyond and Rivers and Seas.

3. Part of a poem called The New Colossus by Emma Lazarus is written on the Statue of Liberty.

4. Little Richard sings Old MacDonald on his kids' album called Shake It All About.

5. Mom likes to watch The Simpsons.

6. My dad reads two newspapers, the Atlanta Constitution and the Wall Street Journal, plus Time magazine.

TEKS 5.21C
ELPS 4C

 **Directions** Write five sentences, each one including one of the following titles: your favorite song, CD, TV show, movie, and book. Punctuate the titles correctly.

1. (song)

_____

_____

2. (CD)

_____

_____

3. (TV show)

_____

_____

4. (movie)

_____

_____

5. (book)

_____

_____

ELPS 4C

Dashes

A **dash** is used to show a break or change in direction in a sentence. (See *Texas Write Source* page 548.)

Example

Sometimes Laura puts grape or cranberry juice—how weird—on her cereal.

Directions ▶ **Add dashes where they are needed in the following sentences. The first one has been done for you.**

1. My brothers read all the Goosebumps books ∧ I love the name *Goosebumps* ∧ by R. L. Stine.

2. Christopher Pike maybe you've heard of him also writes scary books.

3. I must go to the dentist my least favorite thing to do after school.

4. We walked all the way home imagine this wearing our costumes.

5. Gary said and I don't believe it that he finished his homework.

6. Sarah isn't coming I don't know why so don't wait for her.

7. What's that old song Amber was singing it about the bayou?

8. Ben he's so lucky is moving to Florida.

The Next Step **Write four sentences that use dashes correctly. The sentences can tell a story, or each sentence can be about a different topic.**

Parentheses

Parentheses are used to separate words or phrases added to a sentence to make it clearer. (See *Texas Write Source* 548.4.)

Example

The high-speed commuter train (The Coast Flyer) runs every day at 6:00 a.m. and 5:00 p.m.

Directions ▶ Read the following sentences and add parentheses where they are needed.

1. Felicia's father works in Evanston a Chicago suburb.

2. She says that he gets up very early around 4:30 a.m. to catch the train to Evanston.

3. He likes his job working with electricity and living in the suburbs.

4. Sometimes he wires new homes, but often his work is in older homes with outdated wiring.

5. Felicia sometimes worries about dangers bare wires and downed power lines that her father has to handle.

6. She knows that electricity a powerful force can be very dangerous.

7. Her dad tells her he's very careful no daydreaming on the job.

8. Her mother reminds Felicia about his numerous awards for safety.

TEKS 5.21B(i)
ELPS 4C

Punctuation Review 1

The following paragraphs use kinds of punctuation that you have practiced. Use "Editing for Mechanics" on *Texas Write Source* pages 523–549 to help you.

Directions ▶ In the following paragraphs, most of the punctuation marks are missing. Correct the paragraphs by adding commas, apostrophes, semicolons, hyphens, and end punctuation. The first sentence has been done for you.

1   The game of Monopoly is popular now , but it didnt start out

2   that way. Charles Darrow, the inventor, tried to sell the game to

3   Parker Brothers Company but they didnt want to buy it Parker

4   Brothers said Darrows game took too long to play, had mistakes

5   in the instructions and wouldnt sell Darrow had a few Monopoly

6   games made and he paid for them himself Monopoly became very

7   popular so Parker Brothers decided to buy it after all Monopoly

8   became the best selling game of all time in fact, more Monopoly

9   money than real money is printed every year How do you think

10 Charles Darrow would have felt about this

11   One day a businessman in England decided that the game

12 would sell well in that country but he thought local street names

13 were needed Also he decided to have British pounds instead of

14 dollars The Monopoly game is now printed in 26 languages and it

TEKS 5.21B(i)
ELPS 4C

15 is sold in 80 countries Most people who play Monopoly enjoy this

16 slow paced game How can this be Dont people prefer the faster

17 pace of computer games Of course, some do enjoy the speed but

18 millions more like Monopoly

19   I heard there was a tournament at Peters Township Public

20 Library 616 E. McMurray Road McMurray Pennsylvania. The

21 tournament began at 1100 a.m. and ended at 230 p.m. After

22 checking the Internet I discovered there are tournaments across

23 the country. Although the McMurray tournament was only a local

24 contest many tournaments lead to a national competition. To find

25 out more about all these tournaments Im going to write to Hasbro

26 Games 443 Shaker Road East Longmeadow Massachusetts 01028.

ELPS 2C, 4C

Punctuation Review 2

Here's a challenge. This activity is a review of some of the kinds of punctuation you have studied.

Directions ▶ **Some of the punctuation has been left out of the following story. First, read the story aloud, then add the needed punctuation. (The number at the end of each line tells you how many punctuation marks you need in that line.)**

1   Last spring, I visited my grandparents birthplace: *(1)*

2   Fredericksburg, Texas. There are lots of places to go in   *(0)*

3   Fredericksburg Enchanted Rock State Park Fort Martin Scott   *(3)*

4   museums and more. Another place the Plaza of the Presidents   *(3)*

5   honors all the ex presidents who served in World War II. But   *(1)*

6   I want to explain a Fredericksburg tradition—the Easter Fires   *(1)*

7   It dates back to Native American times.   *(0)*

8   European settlers most of the settlers around   *(1)*

9   Fredericksburg were German immigrants built Fredericksburg   *(1)*

10   in an area where Comanche Indians lived. One year, on   *(0)*

11   the night before Easter the settler leaders and the   *(1)*

12   Comanche leaders were having a powwow to decide   *(0)*

13   whether to live in peace or to fight. Small campfires dotted   *(0)*

14   the hillsides around the town One pioneer mother told   *(1)*

15   her children Don't be afraid! The Easter rabbit made the   *(1)*

TEKS 5.21B(i), 5.21B(ii), 5.21C ELPS 4C

16 fires He is boiling your Easter eggs right now! Of course, the   *(2)*

17 campfires were Comanche fires the Comanches were waiting   *(2)*

18 they were waiting as anxiously as the pioneers to hear if a   *(1)*

19 peace treaty would be made.   *(0)*

20 Peace was made. The Meusebach-Comanche Treaty of   *(0)*

21 1847 is one of very few Native American treaties maybe the   *(1)*

22 only one never broken. The Easter Fires are still lit every   *(1)*

23 year and a play is performed to retell the dramatic story.   *(1)*

Directions ▶ **Add the correct punctuation where it's needed in the following dialogue.**

1 What are you doing, Frank Jamal asked.

2 "I'm thinking of titles for my book, song, and movie" said

3 Frank.

4 I like to write funny titles for my stories Jamal said. So,

5 what titles do you have I hope they are funny like mine.

6 "No. My book is about a wolf that gets separated from the

7 pack said Frank. "I'm going to call the book The Lost Wolf Runs."

8 "Hmm that's not too bad. What are your other titles"

9 I'll call my movie Standing Tree, said Frank. I'm still

10 working on a song idea.

ELPS 2C, 4C

Capitalization 1

You know that the first letter of a sentence is always capitalized. Yet other capitalization rules might not be so obvious. This activity will give you practice capitalizing proper nouns that are geographic terms, proper adjectives, and titles used with names. (See *Texas Write Source* 550.1 and 550.3.)

Examples

Proper Nouns That Are Geographic Terms:
My family recently moved here from **Chicago**.
(*Chicago*, the name of a city, is a proper noun.)

Proper Adjectives:
A **Chicago** mayor oversees more people than some state governors do.
(*Chicago* is a proper adjective that modifies *mayor*.)

Titles Used with Names:
For years, Chicagoans kept re-electing **Mayor** Daley.
(*Mayor* is a title connected with a name.)

 **Directions** ▶ **Find and change the words that should be capitalized. The first sentence has been done for you.**

1. Gustavo and I went with _Aaunt Julia to meet _Ggovernor Flood.

2. He came to our town to give a speech about _Mmayor _Ffrost.

3. We live in _Rragener, _Ssouth _Ccarolina.

4. Aunt Julia says _Mmayor Frost is a friend of the _Ggovernor.

5. So, the _Ggovernor came to campaign in the capital city, _Ccolumbia.

6. Once _Aaunt Julia said that the _Ggovernor would go to _Mmars for _Mmayor Frost.

7. My _Aaunt says the _Ggovernor wants to go to _Wwashington, _{DC}d.c., not to _Mmars.

8. She thinks _Ggovernor Flood wants to be the United _Sstates president.

© Houghton Mifflin Harcourt Publishing Company

48

Directions In the following paragraph, capitalize geographic names. See *Texas Write Source* 554.1.

1   Yesterday Rod decided to look at a map of the United States

2   to search for interesting places to visit someday. He started by

3   looking at major rivers. He marked the Mississippi river and the

4   missouri River as must-see destinations and thought about taking

5   a raft trip down the Colorado river through the grand canyon.

6   Then Rod noticed some mountain ranges on the map. He thought it

7   would be fun to hike the appalachian mountains in the East and

8   climb some cliffs in the rocky mountains in the West. He knew

9   he wanted to see the volcanoes of the Cascade mountains. Rod's

10   father had a friend who had just hiked through death valley. Rod

11   wasn't sure he wanted to do that, but he did want to see a desert.

12   Finally, Rod wrote down names of large bodies of water. Floating in

13   great Salt lake sounded like fun. Body surfing in the pacific ocean

14   was also one of Rod's long-time dreams. Rod hoped he could find

15   some friends to paddle canoes with him along the shore of Lake

16   superior in minnesota. When Rod finished his wish list, he realized

17   it might take many years to accomplish all of his travel goals.

The Next Step Write several sentences about famous places you would like to visit. Be sure to properly capitalize your words.

TEKS 5.21A(iii)
ELPS 2C, 4C

Capitalization 4

You know that you should capitalize proper nouns. Proper nouns also include **languages** and names of **organizations**, such as teams and government agencies. (See *Texas Write Source* 550.5 and 552.3.)

Examples

Languages
My father can speak German.

Organizations
He is a member of the Red Cross.

Directions ▸ **Each sentence below contains several capitalization errors. Some errors have to do with languages and organizations. Make the needed corrections. The first sentence has been done for you.**

1. My G̶randfather fought in the K̶orean w̶ar and in w̶orld w̶ar II.

2. In history class, we're studying the r̶evolutionary w̶ar and reading

    about the first President of the United States.

3. The l̶eague o̶f n̶ations was replaced by the u̶nited n̶ations.

4. I've seen the C̶alifornia a̶ngels play B̶aseball in Anaheim Stadium.

5. One common religion in j̶apan is b̶uddhism.

6. Our p̶uerto r̶ican neighbors speak s̶panish at home.

7. My C̶ousin plays baseball with the Texas r̶angers.

8. Asa joined t̶each f̶or a̶merica to help schools and students.

9. Jonathan is j̶ewish, and his family celebrates h̶anukkah.

10. Jamila, who is from k̶enya, knows how to speak s̶wahili.

 TEKS 5.21A(i–iii)
ELPS 4C

Next Step Choose any four of the rules for capitalization shown on *Texas Write Source* pages 550–557. Then write four sentences. Each one of your sentences should use a different rule, but don't capitalize the words that are affected by the rule. Trade with a partner and correct each other's sentences. Be ready to explain the rules you used to make the corrections.

1. _____

_____

_____

_____

2. _____

_____

_____

_____

3. _____

_____

_____

_____

4. _____

_____

_____

_____

ELPS 4C

Plurals 1

There are rules for making **plurals**. (See *Texas Write Source* pages 558 and 560.)

Examples

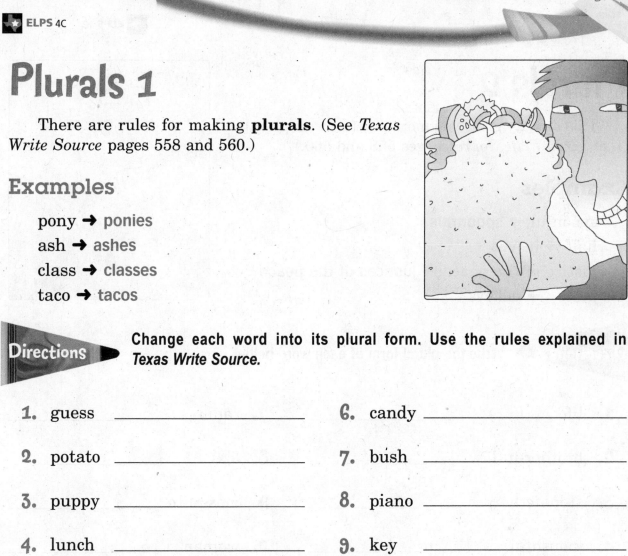

pony ➜ ponies
ash ➜ ashes
class ➜ classes
taco ➜ tacos

Directions | Change each word into its plural form. Use the rules explained in *Texas Write Source*.

1. guess _____

2. potato _____

3. puppy _____

4. lunch _____

5. tomato _____

6. candy _____

7. bush _____

8. piano _____

9. key _____

10. box _____

The Next Step Now develop a "List Poem" using as many of the plural words above as possible. (See the model on *Texas Write Source* page 307.)

_____

_____

_____

_____

_____

ELPS 4C

Plurals 2

This activity gives you more practice with plurals.
(Use *Texas Write Source* pages 558 and 560.)

Examples

spoonful ➜ spoonfuls
half ➜ halves
justice of the peace ➜ justices of the peace
pulley ➜ pulleys

Directions ▶ Write the plural form of each word below.

1. life _____

2. brother-in-law _____

3. stepmother _____

4. mouthful _____

5. roof _____

6. fly _____

7. radio _____

8. fox _____

9. mosquito _____

10. woman _____

11. wolf _____

12. sheep _____

The Next Step Write some silly sentences using all the plurals above that name animals.

_____

_____

_____

_____

TEKS 5.21A(i)
ELPS 2C, 4C

Abbreviations

An **abbreviation** is a shorter way to write a word or a phrase—a shortcut! Most abbreviations begin with a capital letter and end with a period.

Examples

Dr. Bob
(Dr. = Doctor)
1125 Oak Tree Ln.
(Ln. = Lane)

Directions Below are some abbreviations that are often used in writing addresses and times. Match each abbreviation to the word or phrase it stands for.

_____ 1. St.   a. Highway

_____ 2. Pkwy.   b. Terrace

_____ 3. p.m.   c. ante meridiem (before noon)

_____ 4. WY   d. Court

_____ 5. N.   e. Parkway

_____ 6. Dr.   f. post meridiem (after noon)

_____ 7. Sta.   g. Heights

_____ 8. Hwy.   h. North

_____ 9. Ave.   i. Wyoming

_____ 10. Expy.   j. Street

_____ 11. Terr.   k. Drive

_____ 12. Ct.   l. Station

_____ 13. a.m.   m. Avenue

_____ 14. Hts.   n. Expressway

TEKS 5.21A(i)
ELPS 4C

Directions ▶ Some other common abbreviations are listed below. Match each abbreviation to the word or phrase it stands for.

_____ **1.** lb.

_____ **2.** oz.

_____ **3.** etc.

_____ **4.** pd.

_____ **5.** M.D.

_____ **6.** Ms.

_____ **7.** Mrs.

a. doctor of medicine

b. pound

c. paid

d. ounce

e. mistress

f. blend of Miss and Mrs.

g. et cetera (and so forth)

The Next Step Write an address you would find at the top of a letter. Use correct capitalization and punctuation. (See *Texas Write Source* page 564 for more information.)

_____

_____

_____

_____

_____

_____

_____

ELPS 4C

Numbers 1

This activity gives you practice using **numbers** in your writing. See *Texas Write Source* page 566. It explains when to write numbers as numerals and when to write them as words.

Example

Twelve of us turned to chapter 5, but four students opened their books to page 5.

 **Directions**

In the exercise below, some of the numbers need to be changed to numerals, some need to be made into words, and some should be left alone. Refer to the rules on *Texas Write Source* page 566 for additional information and then make your changes. The first sentence has been done for you.

1. There are ~~eleven~~ *11* parts in the school play.

2. 10 people are needed to sing in the chorus.

3. In the play, there are two children who are ten and fifteen years old; all the other characters are adults.

4. 30 of us who are involved with the play will sell tickets.

5. This hilarious comedy has 5 acts and one intermission.

6. If we sell tickets, we'll have to sell fifty tickets to pay for the costumes.

7. We could sell small bags of popcorn for seventy-five ¢ each, if two or three people would agree to sell them.

8. We plan to perform the play on February seven in the evening.

9. 2 afternoon performances are planned for the weekend.

ELPS 4C

Numbers 2

This activity gives you more practice using numbers in sentences. (See *Texas Write Source* page 566 for more information.)

Example

On May **30**, **five** teachers did a short skit.

Directions

In the sentences below, correct the numbers by changing some into numerals and some into words. Then, on the line below each sentence, explain why you made the corrections you made. The first sentence has been done for you.

1. The population of our city is ~~one point three~~ *1.3* million.

   Decimals are written as numerals.

2. Our pie chart showed that only eight percent of our class had the flu.

3. Read chapters one and two, which include pages one through ten.

4. We voted sixteen to nine to get an aquarium.

5. 3 of us brought money to help pay for the aquarium, fish, and food.

6. My birthday party will be Saturday, May six.

TEKS 5.21B(i)
ELPS 4C

Proofreading Practice 1

This activity is a review of using end punctuation and commas. (See *Texas Write Source* pages 523, 524, and 526–532.)

Directions In the following passage, add end punctuation and commas where needed. Capitalize the first letter of each new sentence. The first one has been done for you.

1   Every Thanksgiving holiday, our family gets together at

2   my grandparents' house we eat lots of turkey watch football on

3   TV and talk about which dessert looks the most delicious. This

4   year however we are doing something different. You see Aunt

5   Marta a fitness instructor decided we should be more active. She

6   suggested that we climb Enchanted Rock the Rock is just north

7   of Fredericksburg Texas instead of cooking and eating a rich

8   heavy meal she wants us to pack a lunch. At first several family

9   members mumbled and grumbled, "Hike on Thanksgiving" as time

10   passed more and more people agreed that it was a great idea.

11   Aunt Marta wants to keep us in shape but I just like the idea of

12   doing something fun and different

 **TEKS** 5.21B(ii)
ELPS 4C

Proofreading Practice 2

This activity is a review of using apostrophes, quotation marks, and spacing with dialogue. (See *Texas Write Source* pages 534, 536, and 538.)

Directions In the following passage, add apostrophes and quotation marks where needed. Add missing punctuation to dialogue and show where to begin a new paragraph for a new speaker. The first one has been done for you.

1   Tommy's dream is to become a veterinarian. He became

2   interested in helping animals after he read the story The Boy

3   Who Talked with Animals by Roald Dahl.

4   One day, Lily and Franks dog was not feeling well. Mighty

5   Thor was restless and he didnt want to play ball. Tommy felt

6   Thors belly. It was larger than it should be. "I think Thor's

7   stomach may have flipped," said Tommy with great concern. We

8   need to get him to the vet right now.

9   Tell Mom and get the van ready! Lily shouted, as she helped

10 Thor to the van. Sometimes a large dogs stomach can flip, Tommy

11 explained. Its called bloat. I'm sure the veterinarian can help him.

12   After several hours behind closed doors, the doctor finally

13 appeared. The vets smile said it all.

ELPS 4C

Proofreading Practice 3

This activity is a review of using hyphens, colons, and semicolons. (See *Texas Write Source* pages 540, 542, and 544.)

Directions ▶ In the following story, add hyphens and colons where needed. Replace the comma and conjunction in each compound sentence with a semicolon. The first sentence has been done for you.

1   Attracting birds to your yard is fun, but it is also

2   educational. You can attract birds three different ways provide food

3   for birds, provide water for birds, and provide shelter for birds.

4   If you want your birds to have a year round supply of food,

5   give them a wide variety of foods plant shrubs with berries, plant

6   grasses with seeds, and hang several feeders with seeds.

7   To provide water, you can create a pond in your yard. Ponds

8   should have the following features stones where birds can perch,

9   grasses to provide protection from predators, and fresh water.

10   Some birds make nests in brush piles, but other birds prefer

11 cavities, or holes, in a tree. You can provide a self made nesting

12 box for your birds. Use wood, screws, paint, and other materials to

13 construct a birdhouse.

★ TEKS 5.21B, 5.21C
ELPS 4C

Proofreading Practice 4

This activity is a review of using italics or underlining for titles and emphasis, using quotation marks for titles, using dashes, and using parentheses. (See *Texas Write Source* pages 538.3, 546.1, and 548.)

Directions ▶ In the following passage, underline or add quotation marks to titles. (Remember that you would use italics for underlined titles when using a computer.) Underline one word that you would italicize for emphasis and add dashes or parentheses where needed. The first one has been done for you.

((or) —   ) (or) —

1 Sandra ∧who just moved here from New Mexico∧ has an

2 interesting assignment. She has to brainstorm an idea for a self-

3 help book! Her book is titled Smooth Moves to a New School. The

4 first chapter is called Leaving Old Friends Behind. Sandra says

5 that a big part of moving is feeling lonely and missing old

6 friends and she should know.

7   Sandra's second chapter is called Change Can Be Good. She

8 is going to describe all her new experiences the ones she's had

9 since she moved here in this chapter. She wants to include tips

10 about making and keeping new friends.

11   Sandra's book could be a best-seller with kids at least I

12 think so. She may become a famous writer!

ELPS 2C, 4C

Becoming an Improved Speller

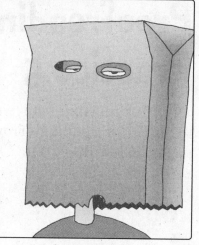

Making up sayings and acrostics can help you remember the spellings of difficult words.

Examples

Use familiar words:
conscience = con + science

Make up an acrostic (funny sentence):
through = Tim had red, orange, ugly, giant hives.

 **Directions**   Try writing sayings or acrostics for four words that give you trouble from the list beginning on *Texas Write Source* page 572. An example has been done for you.

1. *Their, there, and they're all begin with "the."*
   _____

2. _____
   _____

3. _____
   _____

4. _____
   _____

5. _____
   _____

Proofreading Practice 5

After revising your writing assignments, be sure to check for spelling errors. (See *Texas Write Source* pages 568–575.)

Directions ▶ In the following story, label the underlined words "C" for correct, or cross out the word and write the correct spelling above. The first one has been done for you.

1   Last ~~Saterday~~ *Saturday*, we had an ~~advencher~~ *adventure*. Immediately after lunch,

2   we rode to the woods to climb our <u>faverite</u> old maple tree. We had

3   all climbed the tree <u>befour</u>, but this time we <u>desided</u> to see who

4   <u>coud</u> climb to the highest <u>hieght</u>. Ron climbed even higher than

5   <u>any one</u> else, but it was Rita who was the <u>champyon</u> of this

6   race. <u>Unforchunately</u>, she <u>coudn't</u> get down! She didn't <u>realize</u> how

7   high up in that tree she was <u>untill</u> she looked down. Then she

8   panicked. She kept clinging to the branch she was on, even <u>tho</u>

9   she was <u>geting</u> <u>tired</u>. Ron rode <u>straigt</u> back to his house, and his

10   dad called the fire department. An <u>enormus</u> fire engine, with an

11   extension <u>lader</u> and with sirens screaming, rushed <u>to</u> Rita's aid.

12   Despite the <u>excitment</u>, we all learned an <u>important</u> lesson.

ELPS 1E

Spelling Rules 1

Use the basic spelling rules found on *Texas Write Source* page 568 to help you spell *ie* and *ei* words correctly.

Page 528

 **Directions** ▶ Circle the correctly spelled word in each of the pairs below.

1. foreign, foriegn

2. piece, peice

3. cheif, chief

4. weigh, wiegh

5. neice, niece

6. relieve, releive

7. weird, wierd

8. recieve, receive

9. acheive, achieve

10. science, sceince

11. theif, thief

12. height, hieght

Directions ▶ In the following sentences, cross out any misspelled word. Write the correct spelling above the word.

1. Hank and Joe brought thier baseball gloves to the game.

2. The two boys hoped freinds would see them on TV.

3. Neither boy had ever been to a professional baseball game.

4. The two couldn't beleive that they had such good seats.

5. Hank decided to reveiw the lineup for the home team.

6. His favorite player actually grew up in Hank's nieghborhood.

ELPS 1E, 4A, 5B

Spelling Rules 2

Use the silent *e* rule to correctly spell words with suffixes added. If a word ends with a silent *e*, drop the *e* before adding a suffix (ending) that begins with a vowel.

Examples

Josie likes creating (create + ing) computer screen savers.

She is careful (care + ful) to save her changes.

Directions ▸ **Add the suffix indicated to each of the following words.**

1. advise + ing _____

2. hope + ful _____

3. achieve + able _____

4. state + ment _____

5. relate + ing _____

6. care + ing _____

7. continue + al _____

8. create + ive _____

9. advise + ment _____

10. hope + ing _____

The Next Step Write a sentence for each of the following words: *hope + ful, judge + ing, create + ion*. (Remember to spell the new words correctly.)

ELPS 1E

Spelling Rules 3

Words ending in *y* can be tricky to spell. (See *Texas Write Source* 568.3.)

Examples

toy ➜ toys

fly ➜ flies ➜ flying

 **Directions** In the following sentences, correct the misspelled words. The first one has been done for you.

1. Every day Jim ~~trys~~ *tries* to jump over the creek behind the school.

2. The boies are going to play baseball later this afternoon.

3. Emily cryed for joy when she saw her new bike.

4. Jezreel's new puppy is very plaiful.

5. Five ladys and six men from the school board will tour the new school.

6. The principal gave the janitor a new set of keyes.

7. Several countys in the state may build fitness centers.

8. Our neighborhood has five alleyes.

9. Jane keeps two diarys. One is about school, and one is about home.

10. This test will be offered during the next three daies.

The Next Step Write a sentence using each of the following words in its plural form: *journey, anniversary, Friday,* and *library.*

Spelling Rules 4

Words ending in a consonant need special attention. (See *Texas Write Source* 568.4.)

Correct any misspelled words that are underlined in the paragraph below. The first one has been done for you.

1   Both boys and girls know that <u>bating</u> *batting* practice is very

2   important. They know that practice is just a <u>beginning</u> for

3   them. With practice, they will get better at <u>spoting</u> a good pitch

4   and <u>hiting</u> the ball. They also know <u>listenning</u> to the coach

5   is important. Some coaches think players should be <u>attackking</u>

6   the ball all the time. Those coaches must be <u>thinkking</u> such a

7   strategy will score runs. The truth is that a batter must choose

8   wisely which pitch to hit. When a ball is <u>bunted</u>, batters have

9   other special concerns. To send the ball <u>climbbing</u> into the sky,

10   a batter has to see a good pitch coming, swing well, and hit the

11   ball solidly. Batters soon learn they are <u>guardding</u> the plate. Once

12   boys and girls learn to hit the ball, they will be <u>beging</u> to bat all

13   the time.

Spelling Review 1

Look at the underlined words in the following story. Cross out the misspelled words and write the correct spellings above. If a word is spelled correctly, write "C" above it.

1   One September afternoon, Jutta and I quickly changed into

2   old <u>cloths</u> and headed to our <u>freinds'</u> trout pond. Once there, we

3   <u>tackled</u> the easy job of <u>neting</u> 10 trout from the holding tank for

4   our supper that night. Then our friends Karl and Bert <u>usd</u> a

5   rowboat to pull a huge fishnet across the pond. Jutta kept the

6   fish busy by tossing food <u>pellets</u> out in front of the net. With Karl

7   on one side and Bert on the other, they began <u>draging</u> the net

8   toward shore. There, Jutta and I <u>neted</u> the churning, <u>thrashhing</u>

9   fish. <u>Niether</u> of us could <u>believe</u> it—150 trout! Our friends would

10 have a freezer full of fish for the winter. <u>Finaly</u>, we moved all the

11 fish into the large <u>holdding</u> tank. Meanwhile, Karl's mother had

12 finished cleaning the 10 trout and seasoning them for the grill. By

13 then we were all <u>geting</u> hungry and impatient for supper.

Spelling Review 2

Directions **Correct the misspelled words in the paragraph below. The first one has been done for you.**

1. Another name for huge thunderstorm ~~cloudes~~ *clouds* is cumulonimbus.

2. One little boy I know crys when he sees that kind of cloud.

3. The lightning, thunder, and big raindropes frighten him.

4. The highhest clouds, known as cirrus, can be more than eight miles above the earth.

5. A cumulonimbus cloud may be thousandes of feet tall.

6. Scientists can estimate how much a cloud wieghs.

7. Fog is a cloud that is moveing slowly across the ground or just standing still.

8. Hopeing to see better in fog, drivers sometimes use yellow lights.

9. Clouds can cover the sky for several daies.

10. Spoting a tornado in a thundercloud is not always easy to do.

11. The freezeing level for clouds is about six and a half miles above the ground.

12. Above that hieght, clouds are made up of ice crystals.

13. Freindly-looking cumulus clouds mean fair weather.

Sentence Activities

The activities in this section cover three important areas: (1) the basic parts of sentences, (2) common sentence errors, and (3) ways to add variety to sentences. Most activities contain a main practice part, in which you review, combine, or analyze sentences. In addition, **The Next Step** and **Learning Language** activities give you follow-up practice with certain skills.

ELPS 2C, 4C, 5D

Simple Subjects and Predicates

What are the basic parts that every sentence must have? If you answered a **simple subject** and a **simple predicate**, you are right. In each example, the simple subject is underlined once and the verb twice. (See pages 468, 596, and 598 in *Texas Write Source* for more information.)

Examples

Fish swim in the ocean.

Birds fly in the sky.

Directions Read the five sentences below. Find the simple subject in each sentence. Then rewrite the sentences, changing the simple subject. The new subject can be anything you choose, as long as it makes a correct sentence. Circle your new simple subjects. The first one has been done for you.

1. Can fish fly?

   Can a (dog) fly? _____

2. The flying fish doesn't really fly.

   _____

3. Like a glider, the flying fish soars through the air.

   _____

4. Ducks swim in lakes and ponds.

   _____

5. Do ducks fly south for the winter?

   _____

ELPS 4C, 5D

Directions   Read the same five sentences taken from the previous exercise and rewrite the sentences again. This time change the verb instead of the subject. Circle your new verbs.

1. Can fish fly?

_____

2. The flying fish doesn't really fly.

_____

3. Like a glider, the flying fish soars through the air.

_____

4. Ducks swim in lakes and ponds.

_____

5. Do ducks fly south for the winter?

_____

The Next Step Write four sentences about your favorite time of the year. Circle the simple subject and underline the simple predicate.

ELPS 2C, 4C, 5D

Compound Subjects and Predicates

A sentence may have more than one simple subject (a **compound subject**) or more than one simple predicate (a **compound predicate**). In fact, a sentence may even have both a compound subject and a compound predicate. (See *Texas Write Source* pages 469, 596.4, and 598.4.) Remember that another term for *simple predicate* is *verb*.

Examples

Compound Subject: My <u>sister</u> and her <u>friend</u> <u>went</u> to a movie.

Compound Predicate: <u>They</u> <u>ate</u> popcorn and <u>drank</u> soda.

Directions Rewrite each of the following sentences two times. The first time, change the sentence so that it has a compound subject. The second time, change the sentence so that it has a compound predicate. The first one has been done for you.

1. Tracy moved to Arizona.

   Compound Subject: <u>Tracy and Teddi moved to Arizona.</u>

   Compound Predicate: <u>Tracy moved to Arizona and started school.</u>

2. Tracy's grandmother lives there.

   Compound Subject: _____

   _____

   Compound Predicate: _____

   _____

⭐ **ELPS** 4C, 5D

3. Tracy wrote us a letter.

Compound Subject: _____

_____

Compound Predicate: _____

_____

4. Tracy goes swimming every day.

Compound Subject: _____

_____

Compound Predicate: _____

_____

The Next Step
Write one sentence that has a compound subject, one sentence that has a compound predicate, and one sentence that has both. Your sentences can be about Tracy and her family in Arizona, or about anything you like.

1. *Compound Subject:* _____

_____

2. *Compound Predicate:* _____

_____

3. *Compound Subject and Compound Predicate:* _____

_____

_____

TEKS 5.20B
ELPS 2C

Simple and Complete Subjects

Every sentence has a subject. A **simple subject** is the main word in the subject without the words that describe it. The **complete subject** of a sentence includes all the words that tell *whom* or *what* the sentence is about. (See pages 467–468 and 596 in *Texas Write Source* for more information.)

Example

A large and noisy raccoon tipped over the garbage can.

Complete subject: A large and noisy raccoon

Simple subject: raccoon

Underline the complete subject in each sentence. Then circle the simple subject. The first sentence has been done for you.

1. The blue ink leaked all over my shirt.

2. A giant boulder rolled onto the road.

3. The little girl on the bicycle gave me a flower.

4. The old post office has been converted into a museum.

5. My best friend invited me to go roller skating.

6. My dog jumped into the lake to get the ball.

7. Jamal wrote a great poem about the playground.

Learning Language Write two sentences that have a complete subject. Think of another sentence that uses a complete subject and say it aloud to a partner.

TEKS 5.20B
ELPS 2C, 4C

Simple and Complete Predicates

The predicate of a sentence says something about the subject. A **simple predicate,** or **verb,** is the main word in the complete predicate. The **complete predicate** of a sentence includes the verb and all its modifiers. (See *Texas Write Source* pages 467–468, and 598.)

Example

My little brother trained our new puppy.

    Complete predicate: trained our new puppy

    Simple predicate: trained

 **Directions** Underline the complete predicate in each sentence. Then circle the simple predicate (verb). The first sentence has been done for you.

1. Our oak tree (fell) over last night.

2. The man in the white jacket is my uncle.

3. My two sisters hiked ten miles in Big Bend National Park.

4. I ate two bowls of chili for lunch.

5. My science class took a field trip last week.

6. I wore my favorite scarf to school.

7. Last Saturday, my friends and I played football.

Learning Language Write a sentence with a complete predicate about something that happened yesterday. Then think of another sentence and say it to a partner. Tell the partner which word is the verb.

Clauses

A **clause** is a group of related words that has both a subject and a predicate. An **independent clause** expresses a complete thought and can stand alone as a sentence. A **dependent clause** does not express a complete thought and cannot stand alone. (See *Texas Write Source* page 600.)

Examples

Independent Clause: Our old <u>VCR worked</u>.

Dependent Clause: After <u>we</u> <u>fixed</u> the remote control

Directions On the line before each clause, write "D" if it is a dependent clause and "I" if it is an independent clause. Add correct end punctuation for each independent clause. The first one has been done for you.

_____*I*_____ **1.** We got a new VCR.

_____ **2.** When we lost the remote control

_____ **3.** After Max put his peanut butter sandwich in it

_____ **4.** Max is only three

_____ **5.** Since the sandwich was in there

_____ **6.** A million ants crawled into the VCR

_____ **7.** When my dad found out

_____ **8.** Until Max gets older

_____ **9.** The new VCR sits on a high shelf

_____ **10.** Although Max broke the VCR

_____ **11.** Mom says Max is creative

Directions   Make each dependent clause on the previous page into a complete sentence. To do this, add an independent clause. The first one has been done for you.

1. *When we lost the remote control, we didn't know how to start the VCR.*

2. _____

_____

3. _____

_____

4. _____

_____

5. _____

_____

6. _____

_____

The Next Step Write two sentences with a dependent clause at the beginning and two sentences with a dependent clause at the end. Underline the dependent clauses.

TEKS 5.20A(v)
ELPS 2C, 4C

Prepositional Phrases

Prepositions are words that introduce prepositional phrases. A **prepositional phrase** can show location, time, or direction, or provide details. A **prepositional phrase** includes a preposition, the object of the preposition, and any describing words that come in between. (For a list of prepositions, see *Texas Write Source* page 632.)

Examples

He ran **through the doorway**.
(This prepositional phrase includes the preposition *through*, the object *doorway*, and the article *the*.)
Without a doubt, they had the flu.

> **Directions** Read the sentences below. Circle each preposition and underline each prepositional phrase. The number of phrases is given in parentheses.

1. David made a valentine (for) his mom. *(1)*

2. He made it in the shape of a heart on red paper. *(3)*

3. It had a picture of flowers on the front. *(2)*

4. David wrote a poem inside the card. *(1)*

5. It was about all the things his mom does for him. *(2)*

6. He signed his name beneath the poem and put it in an envelope. *(2)*

7. He gave the card to his mom after school. *(2)*

8. She told everyone about the card she got from David. *(2)*

9. She took the card to work and put it on her desk. *(2)*

TEKS 5.20A(v)
ELPS 4C

Directions ▶ Use the prepositional phrases listed below to fill in the blanks of the story.

Around the world	into the air	with each other	in the nets
into a tight circle	In a single day	in front of ships	near people
along the bottom	in the ocean	into the circling fish	

1   Dolphins are some of the most graceful animals that live

2   _____. They can swim as fast as 25 miles per hour

3   and sometimes leap high _____. Dolphins have been

4   seen swimming _____ to catch the bow wave. They

5   work together to force fish _____. The dolphins

6   then take turns dashing _____. By working together,

7   dolphins catch their prey. _____, a dolphin can eat

8   thirty to forty pounds of fish!

9   _____, fishing vessels are a real danger. These

10   boats sometimes use huge nets that drag _____ of the

11   ocean. Dolphins can get caught _____. Fortunately,

12   newer net designs have helped dolphins escape. Dolphins are very

13   curious and like to be _____. Dolphins communicate

14   _____ using clicks, chirps, and actions. One day,

15   scientists hope to communicate with these creatures.

Learning Language Write a sentence using a prepositional phrase about your favorite animal. Think of another sentence using a prepositional phrase and say it to a partner and tell which word is the preposition.

ELPS 2C, 4C

Sentence Fragments 1

The following activity gives you practice correcting one kind of sentence error: **sentence fragments.** A fragment is a group of words that is missing a subject, a predicate (verb), or both. It does not express a complete thought. (See *Texas Write Source* page 470.)

Examples

Sentence Fragments:

Lives at the zoo. (missing a subject)

The animals in that cage. (missing a predicate)

Roaming around. (missing a subject and a predicate)

Directions On each line below, put an "S" if the words that follow are a sentence, or an "F" if they are a fragment. For each fragment, figure out what is missing—the subject, the verb, or both—and write that word on the line to the right of the fragment. The first fragment has been marked for you.

___F___ **1.** A baby alligator to our science class. _____verb_____

_____ **2.** Brought it from the zoo. _____

_____ **3.** It was only about one foot long. _____

_____ **4.** Named her Alice. _____

_____ **5.** Was afraid of the alligator. _____

_____ **6.** Alice afraid of him, too. _____

_____ **7.** Next week, the zookeeper will bring an iguana. _____

_____ **8.** Our teacher animals. _____

_____ **9.** Animal visits make our class fun. _____

_____ **10.** In the afternoon. _____

Directions Go back to the fragments on page 96 and make each one into a complete sentence. Add and underline a subject, a verb, or both, whatever is needed. Use correct capitalization and punctuation. The first one has been done for you.

1. *A baby alligator came to our science class.*

2. _____

   _____

3. _____

   _____

4. _____

   _____

5. _____

   _____

6. _____

   _____

7. _____

   _____

The Next Step Write five sentences about your favorite zoo animal. Make sure at least two of the sentences are sentence fragments. Exchange papers with a classmate and rewrite the fragments so that they are complete sentences.

⭐ ELPS 2C, 4C

Sentence Fragments 2

This activity gives you practice correcting sentence fragments. (See *Texas Write Source* page 470.)

Examples

Sentence Fragments:

needed help to stand due to polio
(missing a subject)

Roosevelt often in a wheelchair
(missing a verb)

Directions ▶ On each line below, put an "S" if the words that follow are a sentence. Put an "F" if they are a fragment. For each fragment, figure out what is missing—the subject, the verb, or both—and write that word on the line to the right of the fragment. The first one has been done for you.

_____F_____ **1.** Franklin Roosevelt president from 1933 to 1945. _____*verb*_____

_____ **2.** Was elected four times. _____

_____ **3.** A lot of other things, too. _____

_____ **4.** Once, he and his friends sailed to an island. _____

_____ **5.** Went there to find buried treasure. _____

_____ **6.** Didn't find any treasure. _____

_____ **7.** Roosevelt something else, though. _____

_____ **8.** Found a nest with four baby birds in it. _____

_____ **9.** He became an avid bird-watcher. _____

_____ **10.** Enjoyed swimming and sailing with his children. _____

_____ **11.** Roosevelt one daughter and five sons. _____

ELPS 4C, 5D

Directions **Read the following paragraph. All the sentences are fragments. Write in the subject or verb that will complete the sentence using the words listed below. You may use the same word more than once. The first one has been done for you.**

Jefferson	helped	had	he
designed	was	liked	sent

                                    was
1   Thomas Jefferson˄president of the United States from 1801 to 1809.

2   The House of Representatives elected him president in 1801 because he

3   and Aaron Burr the same number of electoral votes. In 1803, bought

4   the Louisiana Territory from France. Jefferson then Lewis and Clark to

5   explore the new lands of the Louisiana Purchase. Jefferson interested

6   in knowing what kind of animals lived there and what the land looked

7   like. For many years, tried to keep the country out of the wars going on

8   in Europe. In 1809, retired from public life and went to live at his home,

9   which was known as Monticello. Jefferson this home. He to study many

10   subjects including science, architecture, and music. Wanting to support

11   education, founded the University of Virginia. He to build its first

12   building.

The Next Step Correct each fragment on page 98 so that it becomes a complete sentence.

TEKS 5.15D
ELPS 4C

Run-On Sentences 1

Texas Write Source explains a sentence error called a **run-on sentence**. (See page 471.) You can fix this error by adding end punctuation and a capital letter to split the run-on sentence into two sentences.

Example

Run-On Sentence:
Mark Twain's real name was Samuel Clemens "Mark Twain" was his pen name.

Corrected Sentence:
Mark Twain's real name was Samuel Clemens. "Mark Twain" was his pen name.

Directions ▶ Correct the run-on sentences below by dividing them into two sentences. Use correct capitalization and end punctuation in your new sentences. If the sentence is not a run-on sentence, put a check mark next to it. The first sentence has been done for you.

_____ 1. Mark Twain wrote *Tom Sawyer* and *Huckleberry Finn*. He is one of America's most famous authors.

_____ 2. He was born in Missouri he traveled all over the world.

_____ 3. Before he became a writer, Twain was a riverboat pilot.

_____ 4. He worked on steamboats on the Mississippi River until the river was blockaded during the Civil War.

_____ 5. Twain was also a silver miner in Nevada he was a newspaper reporter, too.

_____ 6. Later, he lived in Hartford, Connecticut, with his family.

5.15D
ELPS 4C, 5F

Run-On Sentences 2

A **run-on sentence** can be corrected by adding a comma and a connecting word to make one correct sentence. (See *Texas Write Source* page 471.)

Example

Run-On Sentence:
Grandma Moses lived to be 101 years old she was a centenarian.

Corrected Sentence:
Grandma Moses lived to be 101 years old**,** **so** she was a centenarian.

 **Correct the run-on sentences below by adding a comma and a connecting word (*and, so, but, yet, or, for,* and *nor*). If the sentence is not a run-on sentence, put a check mark next to it. The first one has been done for you.**

_____ 1. Anna Moses was a famous artist~~,~~ *but* she didn't begin painting until she was 78 years old.

_____ 2. She enjoyed painting scenes near her farm in New York she often gave away her paintings.

_____ 3. One day an art collector saw her paintings in a store window he liked them very much.

_____ 4. He went to her home and bought every painting she had— 15 of them!

_____ 5. Her style of painting was called American Primitive she became famous even in Europe.

TEKS 5.15D
ELPS 4C

Rambling Sentences 1

Texas Write Source explains several different kinds of sentence errors and how to correct them. (See page 471.) This activity gives you practice correcting one kind of sentence error: a **rambling sentence**. A rambling sentence happens when you put too many little sentences together with the word *and*.

 **Directions** Below are two rambling sentences. Correct them by dividing them into as many sentences as you think are needed. Cross out the extra *and*'s, capitalize the first word of each sentence, and use the correct end punctuation. The first part of number 1 has been done for you.

1. Our class went to the art museum, and a man who worked there gave us a special tour. ~~and~~ He told us all about the artists, such as when they had lived and he told us that one artist named Vincent van Gogh had cut off his own ear and Raul asked why, and our guide said that nobody knew for sure and Raul thinks that van Gogh didn't know what he was doing.

2. Maria's mom owns a restaurant called Old Mexico and it's near our school and Maria's mom invited our whole class to come to the restaurant for lunch and our teacher said that we could go, so we went today and we all got to have anything we wanted, and almost everybody had two desserts and it was great!

TEKS 5.15D
ELPS 4C

Rambling Sentences 2

Directions Below are two more rambling sentences. Correct them by dividing them into as many sentences as you think are needed. Cross out the extra *and*'s, capitalize the first word of each sentence, and use the correct end punctuation.

1. Samantha loves the rain and runs outside whenever it rains sometimes she stands in the rain as droplets splash on her face, and she listens to the raindrops hitting the leaves on the trees Samantha tries to imagine what it would be like to be the size of an ant and she doesn't think it would be much fun to be an ant outside in the rain and she thinks it might even be dangerous, and so she's glad that she isn't an ant.

2. The boys' soccer team played well all year and is going to play in the championship game next week and all the students plan to go to the game and cheer for the team and Benington School has had a soccer team for 20 years, but the school has never had a team get into the play-offs before and the whole town is excited and every one of the players has scored at least one goal this year and made an important defensive play and that means the team's success has been due to a combined team effort.

ELPS 4C

Double Negatives

Do not use two negative words, like *not* and *no*, in the same sentence. *Texas Write Source* page 473 explains **double negatives** and shows how to avoid them.

Example

Immigrants **didn't** have **nowhere** to stay at first.
(Change *nowhere* to *anywhere*.)

Directions Correct the double negatives in the following sentences by crossing out or changing the word that is incorrect. If the sentence is correct, put a "C" next to it. The first sentence has been done for you.

_____ 1. A long time ago, people never went ~~nowhere~~ *anywhere* far from home.

_____ 2. There wasn't no reason to leave home.

_____ 3. When Europeans discovered the Americas existed, people began to think about the new land.

_____ 4. Most of these people had never owned no land.

_____ 5. Many years later, poor crops and bad weather caused some people to travel to North and South America to farm.

_____ 6. It was never not easy to clear the land and plant crops.

_____ 7. Many farmers were successful, so others came because they didn't want to be left without no land.

The Next Step Rewrite two of the sentences above that contain double negatives. Correct them in another way this time.

TEKS 5.15D
ELPS 4C

Sentence Errors Review 1

In this activity, you will practice correcting different kinds of sentence errors.

> **Directions** | In the following sentences, there are sentence fragments, run-on sentences, and double negatives. Make the necessary corrections. If the sentence is correct, circle the number.

1. Some classrooms in our school closets for hats and coats.

2. Give tests at least once a week.

3. Joe looked in his backpack, he couldn't find no pencil for the test.

4. My classroom has a tank with three turtles that Arian found and all the students take turns cleaning the tank so that the turtles won't get sick and each day a student is supposed to make sure the turtles are fed.

5. After the turtles were placed in the tank, Rene worried that the turtles wouldn't get no light on weekends.

6. Our brought a light that would hang over the tank.

7. The turtles like to climb on a rock near the light to warm themselves.

8. We that these turtles had to be underwater to swallow their food.

9. The turtles love to eat grasshoppers, but they don't like no spiders.

10. One of the turtles only two inches long.

11. The biggest turtle often sleeps underwater and two other turtles hide in a rock cave and the smallest turtle stays near the other turtles.

12. The whole class watching and caring for the turtles.

TEKS 5.15D
ELPS 4C

Sentence Errors Review 2

In this activity, you will practice correcting different kinds of sentence errors.

 **Directions** ▶ **The paragraph below is full of sentence fragments and run-on sentences. Add the needed words and punctuation to make each sentence complete and correct. The first correction has been done for you.**

1 You probably know that frogs are amphibians. But *here are* some

2 additional facts about frogs. Their eardrums are on the outside

3 of their bodies next to their eyes they can breathe through their

4 skin! Strange creatures. A frog's tongue is attached to its mouth

5 in the front your tongue is attached to the back of your mouth. Is

6 also coated with sticky stuff. Can easily catch insects with it. Most

7 frogs start out as tadpoles some hatch as tiny frogs called froglets.

8 One more fact about frogs. Some frogs *estivate* that means they bury

9 themselves in sand and stay in a sleeplike state when it is hot.

Directions ▶ **The following paragraph includes some rambling sentences and double negatives. Correct them by breaking them into shorter sentences and crossing out incorrect words.**

1 You can watch frogs change from eggs to tadpoles to frogs.

2 All you have to do is go to a quiet pond or a creek in the spring

3 and find some frogs' eggs and then bring them home and watch

4 what happens. An adult can help you find them. Make sure you

TEKS 5.15D
ELPS 4C

5 bring home only a few frogs' eggs and cover them with some of

6 the water in which you found them and also bring some algae

7 and water plants to use in the water with the eggs. The eggs

8 will become little tadpoles in only about a week and when that

9 happens, you should take most of them back to the pond, and you

10 shouldn't never keep more than one or two and also get some

11 fresh water and plants from the pond. At first tadpoles haven't got

12 no legs. You will see the tadpoles grow back legs first, and then

13 they will grow front legs and their tails will go away, too, and by

14 the way, don't worry if your tadpoles never eat nothing while they

15 are losing their tails. That's normal. Now your tadpoles are frogs

16 and you should take them back to where you found them when

17 they were only eggs because grown frogs need to eat living insects

18 and they also need to live with other frogs. Otherwise the frog life

19 cycle can't not go on.

TEKS 5.20C
ELPS 2C, 4C, 5D

Subject-Verb Agreement 1

One basic rule of writing sentences is that the subject and verb must *agree*. Singular subjects take singular verbs. Plural subjects take plural verbs.

Examples

My <u>aunt</u> <u>is</u> from Hawaii.

(*Aunt* and *is* agree because they are both singular.)

<u>Native Americans</u> <u>have</u> their own languages.

(*Native Americans* and *have* agree because they are both plural.)

Directions ▶ **Check the following sentences for subject-verb agreement. If the sentence is correct, put a "C" in front of it. If the subject and verb do not agree, correct the verb.**

_____ 1. Americans speaks more than 100 different languages.

_____ 2. Many people moves to the United States from other countries.

_____ 3. They bring their languages with them.

_____ 4. Most immigrants comes from Mexico and Vietnam.

_____ 5. My friend Annie speak Tagalog.

_____ 6. She is from the Philippines.

_____ 7. Jorge and Marta speaks Spanish.

_____ 8. Some native-born Americans speak two languages.

Learning Language Write a sentence making sure the subject and verb agree. Then say another sentence to a partner that uses the correct subject-verb agreement.

TEKS 5.20C
ELPS 2C, 4C, 5D

Subject-Verb Agreement 2

Subject-verb agreement means that if the subject of a sentence is singular, the verb must be singular, too; if the subject is plural, the verb must be plural. For compound sentences, the subject and verb in both parts of the sentence must agree.

Examples

Megan and Kevin are twins.

Kelly is their sister.

Jake wants to see an action movie, but Rita and Mae prefer a comedy.

Directions ▶ In the sentences below, circle the verbs that agree with the subjects.

1. Every summer the kids in my neighborhood (*put,* *puts*) on a play.

2. Justin and his family (*build, builds*) the stage in their backyard.

3. Isaac or his brother (*is, are*) the director, Julie (is, are) the assistant director, and my friend and I (assist, assists) everyone.

4. Charlie and Juanita (*make, makes*) posters, and (*sell, sells*) tickets.

5. Carla or her sisters (*is, are*) in charge of costumes.

6. Our parents and my uncle Harry (*provide, provides*) popcorn and soda, but I (*bring, brings*) the cups.

7. The actors and the director (*practice, practices*) all summer.

Learning Language Write a compound sentence making sure the subject and verb agree. Then tell a partner another compound sentence that uses the correct subject-verb agreement.

ELPS 4C, 5D

8. On the last weekend in August, we *(is, are)* finally ready.

9. This year's play, written by Isaac and Sharon, *(is, are)* about Robin Hood.

10. Jared or Scott *(is, are)* sure to play Robin.

11. The whole neighborhood *(is, are)* waiting for opening night.

12. The actors *(is, are)* getting nervous.

13. Five teams of professional actors *(donates, donate)* their time as well.

14. Several families *(has, have)* set up chairs for the audience.

15. The local hardware store *(provide, provides)* the lighting for each performance.

16. This year ID Camera Company *(plans, plan)* to make a DVD of the play, and we will *(share, shares)* it with everyone.

The Next Step Imagine that you and your friends are going to put on a play. Write a paragraph telling who would do all the different jobs. Make sure your subjects and verbs agree.

_____

_____

_____

_____

_____

_____

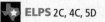 **ELPS** 2C, 4C, 5D

Subject-Verb Agreement 3

Making subjects and verbs agree can be harder when the sentence has a **compound subject**. (Review compound subjects on *Texas Write Source* pages 454 and 469.)

Examples

<u>Luke</u> and <u>Leeann</u> <u>listen</u> to CD's.

<u>Mitchell</u> or the <u>twins</u> <u>ride</u> the scooter.

Directions **In some of the following sentences, the subject and verb do not agree. Correct the verbs in those sentences. Put a "C" in front of any correct sentences. The first sentence has been done for you.**

_____ 1. My mother or sisters ask~~s~~ me questions in Spanish.

_____ 2. Ricki and Rhoda takes me to the movies.

_____ 3. The teacher or the principal make the announcements.

_____ 4. The first baseman or the shortstop bat first.

_____ 5. My brothers and their dog go to the park.

_____ 6. Rick or his sisters takes the trash out.

_____ 7. My family and my school recycles paper.

_____ 8. My mom or my sisters drive me to school.

_____ 9. My sisters or my mom drive me to school.

The Next Step **Using one of the sentences above as a starting point, write a brief paragraph. Use as many compound subjects as you can. Be sure that your verbs agree.**

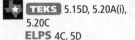 **TEKS** 5.15D, 5.20A(i), 5.20C
ELPS 4C, 5D

Subject-Verb Agreement Review 1

This activity gives you more practice with subject-verb agreement. (See *Texas Write Source* pages 453–454, 469, and 472.)

Directions ▶ Some of the underlined verbs in the draft below do not agree with their subjects. If the verb does not agree, cross it out and write in the correct verb. If the verb does agree, put a "C" above it.

1   The students in my class is making an anthology. An anthology

2 is a collection of writings. There is poems, stories, and drawings in our

3 anthology. Every student have one poem or story in the anthology, and

4 they each have the option to include a drawing.

5   Lisa and Serena loves to make books. They or our teacher

6 remind us each day what needs to be done next. Don or the Haring

7 twins are designing the front cover. They are the best artists in our

8 class. Tina and Mark, with help from the teacher, is laying out the

9 pages on the computer. Kerry's parents, who own a print shop, is going

10 to print and bind the books. The class members gets to go to their shop

11 to see how they make the books.

12   When the books are ready, all the students in the class gets three

13 copies. We plans to sell the extra books to pay for the paper and ink.

Learning Language Write a simple sentence with the correct subject-verb agreement about a story you would write for the book. Then say a compound sentence to a partner about it.

TEKS 5.20A(i), 5.20C
ELPS 4C, 5D

Subject-Verb Agreement Review 2

Directions In the following sentences, write the underlined verb in the singular or plural form to match its subject. If the subject and verb agree, write a "C" above the underlined verb.

1. National park rangers now <u>say</u> that some forest fires are good.

2. A forest fire <u>burn</u> away dry leaves and dead branches.

3. Research <u>show</u> that fire actually <u>helps</u> some plants.

4. For example, the lodgepole pine tree <u>have</u> cones that open only after a fire, and fires <u>clears</u> the brush so their seeds can sprout.

5. Burned trees and plants <u>releases</u> nutrients into the soil.

6. During a fire, plants and animals <u>suffer</u>.

7. Months after a fire, new plant growth <u>mean</u> food for wildlife.

8. Nowadays, firefighters <u>does</u> not try to stop every fire.

9. Sometimes, park rangers or firefighters <u>sets</u> small fires to help prevent big fires, or they <u>let</u> fires in remote areas burn naturally.

10. Forests that are protected from fires <u>has</u> only old trees.

11. In old forests, young trees <u>is</u> not able to get sunlight and <u>grow</u>.

12. An older forest <u>are</u> often devastated by diseases and insects.

13. Some scientists <u>think</u> that forest fires help control these problems.

Learning Language Write a simple sentence with the correct subject-verb agreement about a time you had in a forest. Then say a compound sentence to a partner about it.

ELPS 2C, 4C, 5F

Combining Sentences Using Key Words

You can combine sentences by moving a **key word** from one sentence to another. (See *Texas Write Source* page 479.)

Example

Short Sentences: I lost my book.

It's my math book.

Combined Sentence: I lost my *math* book.

Combine each pair of sentences below by moving a key word from the second sentence into the first. Underline each key word you use. The first one has been done for you.

1. Our teacher found a kitten. It is <u>tiny</u>.

   Our teacher found a tiny kitten.
   _____

2. Our classroom computer crashed. It happened yesterday.

   _____

   _____

3. My dog snores. He snores loudly.

   _____

   _____

4. My friend Willy wrote a story. It's a fantasy.

   _____

   _____

5. We're going to the park. We're going there later.

   _____

   _____

ELPS 4C

Directions Fill in each blank below with any adjective or adverb that makes sense. Then combine each pair of sentences, using the word you filled in as a key word. The first one has been done for you.

1. Dinah opened the door. She opened it _____*slowly*_____.

_____*Dinah opened the door slowly.*_____

2. The door creaked. It creaked _____.

_____

3. Aunt Millie was wearing a hat. The hat was _____.

_____

4. Mason painted his room. He painted it _____.

_____

5. Sarah was wearing a costume. The costume was _____.

_____

6. The cat purred. It purred _____.

_____

7. My mom grows roses. They are _____.

_____

8. Our dog barked at the squirrel. Our dog barked _____.

_____

9. Five cars are parked in the alley. They are parked _____.

_____

★ ELPS 4C, 5F

Combining Sentences with a Series of Words or Phrases 1

You can combine short sentences using a **series of words** or **phrases**. (See *Write Source* page 480.)

Example

Short Sentences: The winters here are too long.
They are too cold. They are also too snowy.

Combined Sentence: The winters here are too long, too cold, and too snowy.

Directions ▶ Combine each group of sentences below, using a series of words or phrases. The first one has been done for you.

1. The river has steep banks. It has a fast current. It has dangerous falls.

   The river has steep banks, a fast current, and dangerous falls.

2. Last night we heard chirping crickets. We also heard hooting owls. We also heard howling coyotes.

   _____

   _____

3. Dad puts tomatoes in his spaghetti sauce. He also puts in mushrooms. He also puts in onions.

   _____

   _____

4. It was cool in the cave. It was dark. It was damp.

   _____

ELPS 4C, 5F

Directions ▶ Fill in the blanks below with any words or phrases that make sense. Then combine each group of sentences. The first one has been done for you.

1. Garter snakes are _____*small*_____. They are _____*colorful*_____.

They are also _____*harmless*_____.

_Garter snakes are small, colorful, and harmless._____

2. Elephants have _____. They also have _____.

They also have _____.

_____

_____

3. Ghosts are _____. They are _____.

They are _____.

_____

_____

4. Aliens from outer space have _____.

They also have _____. They also have _____.

_____

_____

5. Alligators eat _____. They also eat _____.

They also eat _____.

_____

_____

ELPS 4C, 5F

Combining Sentences with a Series of Words or Phrases 2

Texas Write Source page 480 explains ways to combine sentences.

Example

Short Sentences: Jon got a baseball on his birthday. He got a T-shirt. He got a parrot.

Combined Sentence: Jon got a **baseball**, a **T-shirt**, and a **parrot** on his birthday.

 **Combine the following sets of sentences into one sentence. The first sentence has been done for you.**

1. Pizza is cheesy. Pizza is gooey. Pizza is great.

   Pizza is cheesy, gooey, and great.

2. Susan is tall. Susan is thin. Susan is left-handed.

   _____

3. At camp we play baseball. We jump on trampolines. We go rowing.

   _____

4. Marcia goes to the pool. She swims laps. She practices diving.

   _____

5. Nina won an art contest. She won a game of miniature golf. She won a 50-yard dash.

   _____

   _____

ELPS 4C, 5F

Directions ▶ Combine the following groups of sentences into one sentence.

1. Paul mixed some cement. He shoveled it into a wheelbarrow. He pushed it into the garage.

   _____

   _____

2. Franklin chased the ball. He grabbed the ball. He threw the ball to home plate.

   _____

   _____

3. Bob has an old dog. He has a new gerbil. He has a blue parakeet. He has a box turtle.

   _____

   _____

4. Graham read a book about Egypt. He jotted down some notes. He wrote a report about pyramids.

   _____

   _____

5. The blue jay flew against the window. It fell to the ground. It recovered after a few minutes. It flew away in a flash.

   _____

   _____

ELPS 4C

Combining Sentences with Phrases

You can combine sentences by moving a phrase from one sentence to another. (See *Texas Write Source* page 479.)

Example

Two Sentences: Just then the phone rang. The phone is in the hall.

Combined Sentence: Just then the phone in the hall rang.

Directions
For each pair of sentences below, underline a phrase from the second sentence that you can move to the first sentence. Then combine the sentences. The first one has been done for you.

1. Something scary happened last night. It happened <u>in our neighborhood</u>.

   Something scary happened last night in our neighborhood.

2. The lights went out. They went out at about 9:00.

   _____

3. Barney started barking like crazy. Barney is our dog.

   _____

4. I was watching TV until the TV went off. I was watching by myself.

   _____

5. I yelled, "Mom!" I yelled with all my might.

   _____

6. She got a flashlight. She took it out of the closet.

   _____

ELPS 4C

Directions — **Fill in the blanks to complete the following sentences any way you like. Then combine each pair of sentences. The first one has been done for you.**

1. _____Linda_____ went to the Monroe County Fair. She is my

_____cousin_____.

Linda, my cousin, went to the Monroe County Fair.

2. _____ loves chocolate. She is my _____.

_____

_____

3. Mugs is sleeping. He is sleeping _____.

_____

_____

4. I found a box of pennies. I found it _____.

_____

_____

5. _____ took a trip. He went to _____.

_____

_____

6. _____ has a horse. It is _____.

_____

_____

Combining Sentences with Compound Subjects and Predicates

Another way to combine sentences is to move a subject or predicate from one sentence to another. When you do this, you make a **compound subject** or a **compound predicate.** (See *Texas Write Source* page 481.)

Examples

Compound Subject: Carl and Suzanne have pet gerbils.

Compound Predicate: Gerbils run through mazes and use exercise wheels.

 **Directions** ▶ Combine each set of sentences below by using a compound subject or a compound predicate. The first one has been done for you.

1. Farrah is a gerbil. Festus is a gerbil, too.

   Farrah and Festus are gerbils.
   _____

2. Emily takes care of them. Her mom takes care of them, too.

   _____

   _____

3. Farrah plays in the bathtub! Festus plays in the bathtub, too!

   _____

4. Emily and her mom plug the drain. They put in toys.

   _____

   _____

5. The gerbils can exercise. They can sleep.

   _____

ELPS 4C

6. But one day, Emily's mom made a mistake. She left a bath mat over the edge of the tub.

_____

_____

7. Festus grabbed the mat. He climbed out of the tub! He disappeared!

_____

_____

8. Emily and her mom put Farrah in a cage. They went downstairs.

_____

_____

9. Emily searched for Festus. Her mom searched, too.

_____

10. They found Festus in a heat vent. They rescued him.

_____

11. Festus climbed into a tissue box. He was carried to safety.

_____

The Next Step Now imagine that you are Festus! You are telling Farrah all about your adventure. Write some short, choppy sentences telling what you will say to Farrah. Then trade sentences with a partner and try to combine some of each other's sentences. Use any of the different ways you have practiced so far. We have started Festus's story for you.

"I was bored. I tried to find Emily. I crawled into a hole. It was dark! . . ."

ELPS 2C, 4C

Kinds of Sentences 1

There are four kinds of sentences: **declarative, interrogative, imperative,** and **exclamatory.** (See *Texas Write Source* page 475.)

Examples

Declarative Sentence:
The Willis Tower is a famous skyscraper.

Interrogative Sentence:
How many states can you see from the top of this building?

Imperative Sentence:
You must go to the top.

Exclamatory Sentence:
The people on the ground look like ants!

 **Recall a time you had an awesome experience. Maybe you went to the top of a skyscraper, got stuck on the top of a Ferris wheel, or rode a dirt bike for the first time. Write one sentence of each kind about your experience.**

Declarative: _____

_____

Interrogative: _____

_____

Imperative: _____

_____

Exclamatory: _____

_____

ELPS 4C

Kinds of Sentences 2

This activity gives you some practice identifying the four kinds of sentences: **declarative, interrogative, imperative,** and **exclamatory.** (See *Texas Write Source* page 475.)

Directions ▶ Write each sentence below into its proper place in the chart.

Where are you?   The kettle of soup boiled over.

I'm in the kitchen.   Do you need help cleaning the floor?

Come here.   Yes, get the mop please.

Wow, look at the mess!   Ouch, the soup is still hot!

Declarative Sentence:

_____

_____

Interrogative Sentence:

_____

_____

Imperative Sentence:

_____

_____

Exclamatory Sentence:

_____

_____

ELPS 2C, 4C

Types of Sentences 1

Read about **simple, compound,** and **complex** sentences on *Texas Write Source* pages 476–478. See model simple sentences, compound sentences, and complex sentences on those pages.

Examples

Simple Sentence: Charlotte is shy.

Compound Sentence: She is quiet, but she can be daring.

Complex Sentence: I like Charlotte because she is like me.

Directions ▶ On the lines below, write *simple, compound,* or *complex* to identify each sentence. The hardest one has been done for you!

_____ 1. *The True Confessions of Charlotte Doyle* is a book about a wealthy thirteen-year-old girl named Charlotte.

_____ 2. In 1832, Charlotte is supposed to sail from England to Rhode Island with two other families, but the families never show up.

_____ 3. Charlotte decides to sail with the crew alone.

_____ 4. She remains good friends with the captain, until the captain kills two of the crewmen for being traitors.

_____ 5. Charlotte then decides to join the crew and becomes "Mr. Doyle" in the logbook.

_____ 6. During a storm, the first mate is killed with her knife!

complex 7. Avi, the author, wanted to tell his readers that even shy people like Charlotte can become brave.

ELPS 2C, 4C, 5F

Types of Sentences 2

Review the **types of sentences** on *Texas Write Source* pages 476–478. (You may also read about clauses on page 600.)

Examples

Compound Sentence: I have a 4-H cow, and she is a Black Angus.

Complex Sentence: I named her Midnight because she's as black as night.

Rewrite the following simple sentences. First, add an independent clause (another simple sentence) to make a compound sentence. Then add a dependent clause to make a complex sentence.

1. Raul has new skates.

Compound: _____

Complex: _____

_____

2. Anya's school has a computer club.

Compound: _____

Complex: _____

_____

3. Dad cooks Italian food.

Compound: _____

Complex: _____

_____

ELPS 4C

Simple and Compound Sentences

Recall as much as you can about **simple** and **compound sentences**. Then turn to *Texas Write Source* pages 476–477 and carefully reread the section on simple and compound sentences.

Example

Simple Sentences: My sister wants to earn money for camp.
She will wash cars for $3.00 each.

Compound Sentence: My sister wants to earn money for camp, so she will wash cars for $3.00 each.

Think about a time you did something to earn money. Then write four simple sentences about your experience. Finally, combine the sentences so you have two compound sentences. Check the coordinating conjunctions on *Texas Write Source* page 634, and try to use a different one for each sentence. (See page 477 and 526.3 for more on compound sentences.)

Simple Sentences:

1. _____

2. _____

3. _____

4. _____

Compound Sentences:

1. _____

   _____

2. _____

   _____

ELPS 2C, 4C

Compound Sentences

See *Texas Write Source* page 477 for help with combining sentences into **compound sentences**.

Example

Simple Sentences: You could go swimming.
We could take a walk.

Compound Sentence: You could go swimming, or we could take a walk.

 Combine each pair of sentences into one compound sentence. Use a comma and a coordinating conjunction. The first one has been done for you.

1. I made some new friends. They are from other countries.

   I made some new friends, and they are from other countries.

2. Two of them are from Mexico. One is from India.

   _____

3. These friends have different holidays. We celebrate all of them.

   _____

4. Cinco de Mayo is celebrated in Mexico. Divali is celebrated in India.

   _____

   _____

5. I don't speak Spanish or Marathi. My friends speak English.

   _____

The Next Step Write a short story about a holiday or custom your family observes. Check to see if any of your short sentences could be combined into compound sentences. Change them.

★ **TEKS** 5.20A(vii)
ELPS 2C, 4C

Complex Sentences 1

One way to combine simple sentences is to make **complex sentences.** You connect two ideas with a **subordinating conjunction.** Subordinating conjunctions introduce the dependent clauses in complex sentences.

Example

Many French people settled in Canada **while** people from other parts of Europe settled in the United States.

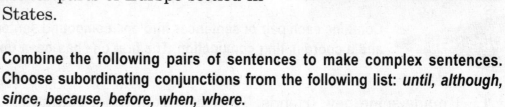

Directions ▶ **Combine the following pairs of sentences to make complex sentences. Choose subordinating conjunctions from the following list:** *until, although, since, because, before, when, where.*

1. Millions of Jewish people left Russia. They faced prejudice there.

   _____

   _____

2. People from Great Britain found it easy to adjust to the United States. They already spoke English.

   _____

   _____

3. Most Irish immigrants came during the 1800s. There was a famine in Ireland.

   _____

   _____

TEKS 5.20A(vii)
ELPS 4C

Directions **Read the paragraph below. Then find and copy the four complex sentences. Finally, circle the subordinating conjunctions.**

When immigrants came to this country in the early 1900s, the first thing many of them saw was the Statue of Liberty. Then they knew that their long sea voyage was over. Before the immigrants were allowed into the United States, they had to talk to government agents. Immigrants then had to stand in another line where a doctor would examine them. They were not sure they could stay, until the agents gave them permission to enter the country.

1. _____

_____

_____

2. _____

_____

_____

3. _____

_____

_____

4. _____

_____

_____

Learning Language Now tell a partner each sentence above as if it were two sentences. (Take out the subordinating conjunction.) Then write a complex sentence using a subordinating conjunction about someone you know from another country. Finally, think of another complex sentence that uses a subordinating conjunction and say it to a partner.

 **ELPS** 2C, 4C, 5D

Complex Sentences 2

One way to combine sentences is to make **complex sentences.** And one way to make complex sentences is with **relative pronouns.** (See *Texas Write Source* page 478 and 614.1.)

Example

Danny, **whose** brother is in our class, will bring a present.

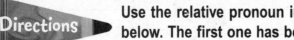
Directions   Use the relative pronoun in parentheses to combine each pair of sentences below. The first one has been done for you.

1. My sister Michelle is having a party. Her birthday is today. *(whose)*

   My sister Michelle, whose birthday is today, is having a party.

2. These cupcakes are for the party. She made them herself. *(which)*

   _____

   _____

3. Her best friend is coming. Her friend lives in Brighton. *(who)*

   _____

   _____

4. I helped put up the decorations. They are in the backyard. *(that)*

   _____

   _____

TEKS 5.20A(v)
ELPS 2C, 4C

Expanding Sentences with Prepositional Phrases

You can add interesting information and details to your writing by using **prepositional phrases**.

Example

Basic Sentence:
The man was taking a nap.

Expanded with Prepositional Phrases:
The man **with the shaggy, brown dog** was taking a nap **under a tree**.

Directions ▶ **In the sentences below, add a prepositional phrase from the list below.**

| from their fishing boats | in the city | during the fall migration |
| of the tropics | with their cheery cheeping | of their apartment buildings |

1. The red and black scarlet tanager is a bird _____*of the tropics*_____.

2. Common birds _____ are English sparrows.

3. Some people like to raise pigeons in cages located on the rooftops

   _____.

4. Parakeets _____ entertain many people.

5. After flying all day _____, geese will often land in grain fields to eat and rest.

6. Seagulls eat what fishers throw back _____.

Learning Language Write a sentence about butterflies using a prepositional phrase. Then think of another sentence using a prepositional phrase and say it to a partner.

Sentence Variety Review

Directions ▶ Identify the following sentences as *declarative, interrogative, imperative,* or *exclamatory.*

_____ 1. Open the umbrella before we get rained on.

_____ 2. How much rain can fall in one hour?

_____ 3. The record rainfall of 12 inches in one hour occurred in Hawaii.

_____ 4. Wow, that was loud thunder!

_____ 5. Did you see that flash of lightning?

_____ 6. The storm clouds are full of lightning.

_____ 7. Let's find some shelter.

_____ 8. I am really scared!

Directions ▶ Identify the following sentences as "simple," "compound," or "complex."

_____ 1. After Jon signed his test, he handed it to the teacher.

_____ 2. His teacher sent the tests to the central office, and other tests were sent from other classrooms.

_____ 3. Students' tests were scanned by a super-fast computer.

_____ 4. When the computer finally stopped, all of the tests had been scored and sorted.

_____ 5. The tests were returned to the school the following day.

Language Activities

Every activity in this section includes a main practice part in which you learn about or review the different parts of speech. Most of the activities also include helpful handbook references. In addition, **The Next Step** and **Learning Language,** which are at the end of most activities, encourage follow-up practice of certain skills.

ELPS 2C, 4C

Nouns

A **noun** names a person, a place, a thing, or an idea. (See *Texas Write Source* page 604.)

Examples

Person: mom, Bob, athlete, musician

Place: kitchen, Idaho, park, harbor

Thing: cup, July, truck, highway

Idea: courage, friendship, freedom

Directions  Do you ever get your words mixed up? Sam Goldwyn, a famous early movie maker, used to do that all the time. Below are some of the humorous things Sam Goldwyn said. Circle all the words used as nouns. (Don't circle pronouns.) The number after each sentence tells you how many nouns the sentence has. The first sentence has been done for you.

1. "The (scene) is dull; tell him to put more (life) into his (dying)." *(3)*

2. "For your information, I would like to ask a question." *(2)*

3. "It's spreading like wildflowers!" *(1)*

4. "You've got to take the bull by the teeth." *(2)*

5. "This new bomb is dynamite." *(2)*

6. "When I want your opinion, I'll give it to you." *(1)*

7. "This book has too much plot and not enough story." *(3)*

8. "Every director bites the hand that lays the golden egg." *(3)*

9. "I never put on a pair of shoes until I've worn them five years." *(3)*

10. "Look how I developed John Hall: He's a better leading man than

    Robert Taylor will ever be—someday." *(3; each name counts as 1 noun)*

ELPS 4C

Directions Below are some more "not quite right" things that different people have said. Again, circle all the words used as nouns.

1. "That guy's out to butter his own nest." *(2)*

2. "You are out of your rocker." *(1)*

3. "I'd like to have been an eardropper on the wall." *(2)*

4. "It's time to swallow the bullet." *(2)*

5. "I'm sticking my neck out on a limb." *(2)*

6. "That's a horse of a different feather." *(2)*

7. "You buttered your bread, Now lie in it!" *(1)*

The Next Step Can you figure out what these people meant to say? Rewrite the sentences above so that they are correct. Circle the nouns in your sentences. The first one has been done for you.

1. *That guy is out to feather his own nest.*

2. _____

3. _____

4. _____

5. _____

6. _____

7. _____

ELPS 2C, 4C

Common and Proper Nouns

A **common noun** is any noun that does not name a specific person, place, thing, or idea. Common nouns are not capitalized. A **proper noun** names a specific person, place, thing, or idea. Proper nouns are capitalized. (See *Texas Write Source* pages 440, 604.1, and 604.2 for more information.)

Examples

Common Nouns: name   book   holiday

Proper Nouns: Maria   Memorial Day   Texas

> **Directions** ▶ Underline each word used as a noun in the sentences below; then write "C" above each common noun and "P" above each proper noun. (Notice that the number of nouns is given in parentheses after each sentence.) The first noun has been marked for you.

1   <u>Juan</u> bought a bike from Green's, a hardware store in the

2   neighborhood. *(5)* He bought a secondhand bike, and it seemed to

3   be in very good condition. *(2)* He bought the bike on Saturday and

4   rode it around on Sunday, but on Monday the handlebars got very

5   loose. *(5)* On Tuesday he took his bike back to the store and told

6   Mr. Green, the owner, about the handlebars. *(6)*

7   Mr. Green got out his wrench and a couple of bolts and fixed

8   the handlebars right away! *(5)* Now Juan thinks his secondhand

9   bike is better than all the new bikes at Green's. *(4)*

⭐ **ELPS** 1E, 3B, 4C

Directions Look around you and notice all the persons, places, things, and ideas. Then make two lists—one of proper nouns and one of common nouns. See how many nouns you can spot!

Proper Nouns	Common Nouns
_____	_____
_____	_____
_____	_____
_____	_____
_____	_____
_____	_____
_____	_____
_____	_____
_____	_____
_____	_____

Learning Language Tell a partner a sentence that uses one common and one proper noun. Then share your sentence with the class.

 **TEKS** 5.20A(ii)
ELPS 2C, 4C

Collective Nouns

A **collective noun** names a group of persons or things. For example, a football *team* has 11 players. There are 12 eggs in a *dozen*. Several kittens form a *litter*.

Examples

class	audience	committee
family	jury	company

Directions Read the following nouns. Write "C" on the line provided if the noun is a collective noun.

1. crowd _____ *C* _____

2. pants _____

3. swarm _____

4. flock _____

5. birds _____

6. colony _____

7. band _____

8. firefighter _____

9. herd _____

10. army _____

11. choir _____

12. kindness _____

Learning Language Write about some animals you saw at the zoo. Use collective nouns in your paragraph. Then tell your partner about the animals you saw. Ask your partner to identify the collective nouns you used. (Remember that collective nouns usually take singular verbs.)

_____

_____

_____

_____

_____

ELPS 2C, 4C

Concrete and Abstract Nouns

Concrete nouns name things that can be touched or seen. **Abstract nouns** name things that cannot be touched or seen. (See *Texas Write Source* 604.3–604.4.)

Examples

Concrete Nouns: flower   cake   Mr. Taylor

Abstract Nouns: joy   April   poverty

Directions ▶ Sort the nouns below into concrete and abstract nouns. Write each noun in the correct column. Then add one noun of your own to each list.

question	happiness	opinion	thumbs
horse	book	day	liberty
teeth	plot	years	sun
path	egg	nest	trust

Concrete Nouns   **Abstract Nouns**

_____   _____

_____   _____

_____   _____

_____   _____

_____   _____

_____   _____

_____   _____

ELPS 4C, 5G

 In the sentences below, underline the nouns and label them "C" for concrete or "A" for abstract. The first one has been done for you.

       C   A   C

1. The <u>boy</u> had a <u>question</u> for his <u>teacher</u>.

2. All the students listened to the answer.

3. Hitting a baseball well is not easy.

4. Alex says happiness will be getting the cast off his arm.

5. That girl has very good table manners.

6. A loose tooth can cause pain and frustration.

7. The builders will finish the bridge in three months.

The Next Step Write two sentences, each using one concrete noun and one abstract noun. An example has been done for you. (You may choose to use some of the nouns on the previous page.)

1. _Today in class, we talked about democracy._

2. _____

_____

_____

3. _____

_____

_____

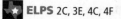 ELPS 2C, 3E, 4C, 4F

Singular and Plural Nouns

A **singular noun** names one person, place, thing, or idea. A **plural noun** names more than one person, place, thing, or idea. (See *Texas Write Source* page 606.)

Examples

Singular Nouns: sister   dog   car

Plural Nouns: sisters   dogs cars

Directions   Underline each word used as a noun. (Don't underline pronouns.) The number of nouns is given in parentheses. Label each noun "S" for singular or "P" for plural. The first sentence has been done for you.

1. My little <u>brother</u> eats <u>oatmeal</u> for <u>breakfast</u> every weekday <u>morning</u>. *(4)*
              S   *S*   *S*   *S*

2. My mom eats cornflakes and pastries or muffins. *(4)*

3. She drinks two cups of coffee, too. *(2)*

4. On weekends we have pancakes, waffles, or scrambled eggs. *(4)*

5. Danny eats his pancakes right after they come off the griddle. *(3)*

6. Our grandparents eat a big breakfast every day. *(3)*

7. They make eggs, sausages, fried potatoes, and cinnamon rolls. *(4)*

8. When Danny goes to visit them, they make oatmeal for him. *(2)*

The Next Step   Write a paragraph about breakfast. Your paragraph could be about what you eat for breakfast, what you would like to eat for breakfast, or the weirdest breakfast you can imagine. When you finish, trade paragraphs with a partner. Underline all the nouns in each other's paragraph. Then label each noun "S" for singular or "P" for plural. Check your partner's work.

⭐ ELPS 2C, 3E, 4C, 4F

Gender of Nouns

The **gender** of a noun means that something is masculine, feminine, neuter, or indefinite. (See *Texas Write Source* 606.3.)

Examples

Masculine:	boy
Feminine:	girl
Neuter:	closet
Indefinite (male or female):	child

 **Directions** In the following sentences, underline and identify the nouns as "F" for feminine, "M" for masculine, "N" for neuter, or "I" for indefinite. The first sentence has been done for you.

1. That <u>boy</u>'s favorite <u>clothes</u> are <u>jeans</u> and a <u>sweatshirt</u>.
   - *(M above "boy", N above "clothes", N above "jeans", N above "sweatshirt")*

2. Girls sometimes have mirrors in their lockers.

3. Parents want their children to be happy.

4. Gophers dig holes in the ground.

5. The pilot of the plane announced a delay for the afternoon flight.

6. All of the students groaned because they would have to wait two more hours.

7. The class was the last one to arrive at the national science fair.

8. Mr. Acker, our English teacher, has two daughters, one niece, and three

   sisters.

9. Sometimes the grandson of a king inherits the kingdom.

The Next Step Write a paragraph about your friends. Exchange papers and underline all the nouns. Then label each noun "M" for male, "F" for female, "N" for neuter, and "I" for indefinite. Check your partner's work.

★ **ELPS** 2C, 4C

Uses of Nouns

Nouns can be used in different ways in sentences. You've had lots of practice using **subject nouns**, which are nouns used as the subject of a sentence. But you also need to know how to use **predicate nouns** and **possessive nouns**. (Read about all three uses on *Texas Write Source* page 608.)

Examples

Subject Noun: My sister went to the library.

Predicate Noun: My sister is an artist.

Possessive Noun: My sister's friends like me.

Directions ▶ **In the sentences below, label all the underlined nouns. Write an "S" above the noun if it is a subject noun, a "P" if it is a predicate noun, and a "POS" if it is a possessive noun. The first sentence has been done for you.**

1. A beagle is a friendly dog.

2. The party will be a surprise.

3. Jeremy's cat is a Siamese.

4. Marla's favorite sport is baseball.

5. Jordan became an editor.

6. The winner was Suzanne.

7. Blake knows Lydia's brother.

8. The book's author signed my copy.

9. Our school's track team won the championship.

10. My best hiding place is the attic.

★ ELPS 4C

Directions Above each underlined noun, write "S" if it is a subject noun, "P" if it is a predicate noun, and "POS" if it is a possessive noun. Draw an arrow from each predicate noun to the subject it renames. The first two nouns have been done for you.

The Frog's Tail (*a West African folktale*)

1   In the beginning, Frog was the only animal that didn't have a

2   tail. The other animals teased him. They said Frog was a freak. So

3   Frog begged Nyame, who had made all the animals, to give him a tail.

4   Nyame gave Frog a tail. In return, Nyame said Frog must be

5   Nyame's guard. Frog's job was to guard Nyame's magic well. Nyame

6   told Frog that when it didn't rain for a long time, the other wells would

7   dry up. When that happened, Frog should let all the animals come and

8   drink at Nyame's well.

9   Well, Frog became a bully. Not only did he have a tail, he also had

10   an important job. Soon the rain stopped. All the other wells dried up.

11   The animals came to Nyame's well. But Frog remembered how

12   they had made fun of him, and he wouldn't let them drink.

13   When Nyame heard what Frog had done, he took Frog's tail away.

14   Ever since then, young frogs have tails, but they lose them as they

15   grow up.

ELPS 2C, 4C

Nouns as Objects

A noun is a **direct object** when it receives the action of the verb. A noun is an **indirect object** when it names the person to whom or for whom something is done. A noun is an **object of a preposition** when it is part of a prepositional phrase. (See *Texas Write Source* 608.4 for more information.)

Examples

Direct Object:	Dennis rides his bike.
Indirect Object:	He gave Wendy a ride.
Object of a Preposition:	They rode to the market.

Directions   **Look at the following sentences and the circled nouns in each. Then label each noun according to which kind of object it is. The first one has been done for you.**

1. Yelena wrote a funny (letter.)   *direct object*

2. Yelena wrote (Mike) a funny letter. _____

3. Yelena wrote a funny letter to (Mike.) _____

4. Mom took (me) to the dentist. _____

5. The teacher wrote on the (chalkboard.) _____

6. Mr. Marple asked (Rhonda) to mow the lawn. _____

7. Dr. Fine gave some (medicine) to me. _____

8. Our dog jumped into the swimming (pool.) _____

9. Peggy cooked (dinner) for the whole family. _____

10. Ty drew (Carla) a picture. _____

 ELPS 3E, 3F, 4C, 5F

Directions Now write three sentences of your own. Each one should contain a noun used as a different kind of object. Your sentences may contain more than one kind of object. *Special Challenge:* You may want to include compound objects in your sentences, just as you sometimes use compound subjects. Check out this example:

(object of a preposition)   *(direct object)*

With her new <u>pen</u>, Yelena wrote <u>Mike</u> and <u>Maggie</u> a funny <u>letter</u>.

(compound indirect object)

Note: Don't underline or label the objects in your sentences yet.

1. _____

_____

_____

_____

2. _____

_____

_____

3. _____

_____

_____

The Next Step When you're finished, exchange your work with a classmate. Find and label the nouns your partner used as objects. Did your partner write at least one example of each kind of object?

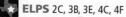ELPS 2C, 3B, 3E, 4C, 4F

Person of a Pronoun

The **person of a pronoun** indicates the point of view of a story. (Read about person of pronouns on *Texas Write Source* pages 445 and 610.3–610.5.)

Examples

First-Person Point of View:
I cleaned and scrubbed the cottage all day.

Second-Person Point of View:
You two will go to the ball to meet the prince.

Third-Person Point of View:
She had to leave the ball by midnight.

Directions In the following sentences, underline the personal pronouns. The number of pronouns in each sentence is in parentheses. Above each pronoun, write a 1, 2, or 3 to show whether it is a first-person, second-person, or third-person pronoun. The first sentence has been done for you.

1. *1*
   I heard that the prince invited everyone in the kingdom to the ball. *(1)*

2. My stepmother said, "You stay here and clean. They will go to the ball." *(3)*

3. They left a little later. *(1)*

4. My fairy godmother appeared, and suddenly I became a princess. *(2)*

5. I was thrilled to meet the prince, and he was happy to meet me. *(3)*

6. At midnight, I ran from the ball, leaving the prince wondering who I was. *(2)*

7. He found one of my glass slippers and began searching for the one he loved. *(3)*

8. He finally found me, and we lived happily ever after. *(3)*

The Next Step Rewrite another fairy tale from a first-person point of view. Share your story aloud with a partner. Have your partner underline each pronoun and identify the point of view.

Number of Pronouns

Review the personal pronoun chart on *Texas Write Source* page 612. Notice the personal pronouns *you, your,* and *yours* can be **singular** or **plural**.

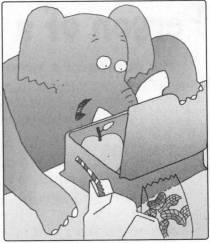

Examples

Singular: I forgot **my** sandwich. Mary, **you** can buy **your** lunch.

Plural: Bill and Mary, when the cooks serve tacos on Friday, **they** offer a special discount. **You** can buy two for the price of one.

Directions ▶ In the following story, underline the personal pronouns. Above each pronoun, write "S" for singular and "P" for plural.

1   One day, my friends and I decided to build a sand castle. We

2   had seen amazing pictures from contests, and we thought we could

3   build a simple one. I told my friends that we would need buckets

4   and shovels. They were already at the beach when I arrived.

5   I saw a hot-dog stand run by a man from our neighborhood.

6   He waved at us, and we waved back. We started to dig in the

7   sand and pile it up. My friends began carving towers and walls.

8   Although they had never done this before, their castle looked great.

9   They even put a moat around it, and then they put a drawbridge

10   across the moat. My friends Jill and Serena said, "Would you

11   go buy us some hot dogs and something to drink?" We enjoyed

12   building our castle, and we later saw it wash away in the tide.

ELPS 2C, 4C

Subject and Object Pronouns

A **pronoun** is a word used in place of a noun. A **subject pronoun** is used as the subject of a sentence. An **object pronoun** is used after an action verb or a preposition. (See *Texas Write Source 612.1–612.2.*)

Examples

Subject Pronoun: I like movies.

Object Pronoun: Sheila asked if Bob likes **them**.

 **Directions** **Each sentence below contains a subject pronoun, an object pronoun, or both. (Some sentences contain three or four pronouns.) Underline and label each subject pronoun "S" and each object pronoun "O." The first sentence has been done for you.**

1. Sheila and I̱ went to a movie.

2. She liked it, but it was too scary for me.

3. After the movie, Sheila's parents, Mr. and Mrs. Daly, took us to a bakery for cupcakes.

4. "You can have any flavor, girls," Mrs. Daly said.

5. "You get a cherry, I will get lemon, and we can share," Sheila said.

6. "Mark is sick," Mrs. Daly said. "We will get a cupcake for him, too."

7. Sheila reminded her that he likes vanilla.

8. "Hey, what about me?" Mr. Daly asked.

9. "No cupcakes for you; you are on a diet!" Mrs. Daly answered.

 **Directions** In each sentence below, cross out the subject. Replace it with the correct subject pronoun: *he*, *she*, *it*, or *they*. The first one has been done for you.

She
1. ~~Sheila~~ liked the movie.

2. The movie was funny.

3. After the movie, Mr. and Mrs. Daly picked up Sheila and Sue.

4. Mrs. Daly bought cupcakes.

5. Sheila got a cupcake for Mark.

6. Mark likes vanilla cupcakes.

7. Mark thanked Sheila.

The Next Step All of the sentences above, except one, contain a noun or noun phrase that can be replaced with an object pronoun. (Remember, an object pronoun is used after an action verb or a preposition.) Replace each noun or noun phrase with the correct object pronoun (*him*, *her*, *it*, or *them*). The first sentence will look like this:

1. Sheila liked it.

2. _____

3. _____

4. _____

5. _____

6. _____

7. _____

ELPS 2C, 4C

Possessive Pronouns

A **possessive pronoun** shows ownership. Some possessive pronouns function as adjectives. These include the words *my, our, his, her, their, its,* and *your.* Other possessive pronouns can stand alone. These include *mine, ours, hers, his, theirs,* and *yours.* (See *Texas Write Source* 612.3.)

Examples

My cat likes to sit on top of the refrigerator.

This book is mine, and that one is hers.

> **Directions** Underline the possessive pronouns in the following sentences. The first sentence has been done for you.

1. Did <u>your</u> mom take <u>our</u> videos back to the store?

2. When its wheels spin, it whistles.

3. Their cat wriggled out of its collar.

4. I will give my book report right after you give yours.

5. Her house is farther from school than ours.

6. Are these markers yours or his?

7. His cousins like our school better than they like their own.

8. Our team has more players than your team has.

9. Her class has a different lunch hour than my class has.

10. That school is theirs, and it has its own swimming pool.

11. My project will be finished before yours is finished.

ELPS 4C, 5E

 **Directions** ▶ Cross out each underlined word or phrase below, and replace it with the correct possessive pronoun. The first one has been done for you.

1. Tim is taking ~~Tim's~~ *his* dog for a walk.

2. Our teacher showed us pictures of <u>our teacher's</u> vacation.

3. Mohan and Jon won first prize for <u>Mohan and Jon's</u> science project.

4. Whose poem is longer, <u>Philip's</u> or <u>Marie's</u>?

5. The bird is building <u>the bird's</u> nest.

6. The party will be at <u>my family's</u> house.

7. Is this <u>Taylor's</u>?

8. Taylor thought it was <u>Taylor's</u>.

9. The storm left damaged buildings in <u>the storm's</u> wake.

10. Those skates are <u>my skates</u>.

The Next Step Write three sentences of your own that correctly use possessive pronouns.

1. _____

_____

2. _____

_____

3. _____

_____

★ **TEKS** 5.20A(vi)
ELPS 2C, 2I, 3B, 3E, 4C

Indefinite Pronouns

An **indefinite pronoun** refers to people or places that are not named or known. Here are some indefinite pronouns: *all, another, any, anybody, anyone, anything, both, each, each one, either, everybody, everyone, everything, few, many, most, much, neither, nobody, none, no one, nothing, one, other, several, some.*

Example

Something special is planned for the party.

Directions Underline all the indefinite pronouns in the following sentences. Then pick three indefinite pronouns and use them in written sentences.

1. <u>All</u> of the cookies are gone.

2. Most of the ice cream is gone, too.

3. We need a cowboy hat for the play, but nobody has one.

4. Everybody is studying for the test.

5. Mom said, "Either of you can take the trash out."

6. One of us will have to do it.

7. When we start playing volleyball, anything can happen.

8. All of the players do their best.

9. None of my friends are on my team.

10. The chair got wet because somebody left the window open.

Learning Language Tell a partner about something mysterious that happened. Use indefinite pronouns. Then have your partner retell the story to you, making it spookier.

 **TEKS** 5.20A(vi)
ELPS 2G, 3E, 4C

Directions ▶ Complete each of the following sentences by writing an indefinite pronoun on the line. Choose from the following list of indefinite pronouns.

someone	anyone	no one	everyone
somebody	anybody	nobody	everybody
somewhere	anywhere	nowhere	everywhere
something	anything	nothing	everything

1. Have you seen my book? I can't find it _____.

2. Do you think _____ hid it from you?

3. I can't fit _____ else in my backpack.

4. _____ in our class likes to read.

5. I can tell _____ likes this tea. The pitcher is still full!

6. _____ is going wrong today! First I failed my test, and

   then I realized I was wearing two different shoes on my feet.

7. The nurse wants _____ with a cold to go home.

8. I was going to tell you _____, but I forgot what it was.

Directions ▶ Now write a sentence for each of the indefinite pronouns listed below.

1. several _____

   _____

2. most _____

   _____

Learning Language Tell a partner about a recent school event. Use an indefinite pronoun.

ELPS 2C, 4C

Relative and Demonstrative Pronouns

Relative pronouns such as *who, whose, whom, which, that, whoever, whomever, whichever, whatever,* and *what* connect one part of a sentence with another word in the same sentence. **Demonstrative pronouns** such as *this, that, these,* and *those* point out nouns without naming them. (See *Texas Write Source* 614.1 and 614.3.)

Examples

Relative Pronoun: Students **who** will help recycle must sign up today.

Demonstrative Pronoun: Put the shelves here. **These** will hold the glass.

Directions ▶ Underline the relative and demonstrative pronouns below. Identify them by using an "R" or a "D." The first one has been done for you.

___R___ **1.** Aluminum cans, <u>which</u> are everywhere, should be recycled.

_____ **2.** Recycling has caught on because this saves money.

_____ **3.** A lot of electrical power that aluminum plants use is needed to first get the metal from the ore.

_____ **4.** An aluminum company employee whose job deals with recycling says that 90 percent less power is used to melt used cans.

_____ **5.** Used cans are wanted because those are an important source for aluminum.

_____ **6.** Some students who want to earn money and clean up the land pick up as many cans as possible.

_____ **7.** Some states that hope to reduce litter will pay five or ten cents for each returned can.

_____ **8.** Many states require a deposit on every new can and these have set up recycling centers in every town.

_____ **9.** Whoever grabs a garbage bag and picks up cans off the street can earn some extra money.

 **ELPS** 2C, 4C, 5D, 5E

Pronoun-Antecedent Agreement 1

Antecedent is the name for the noun that a pronoun replaces. Each pronoun in your sentences must agree with its antecedent. (See *Texas Write Source* page 445.)

Examples

My **sister** had fun at **her** first clown camp.
(The pronoun *her* and its antecedent *sister* are both singular and feminine, so the pronoun and its antecedent agree.)

Aunt Marietta and **Uncle Bill** join in the clown parade in **their** city.
(The pronoun *their* and its antecedent *Aunt Marietta* and *Uncle Bill* are both plural, so the pronoun and its antecedent agree.)

Directions ▶ Circle the pronouns in each of the following sentences. Draw an arrow to each pronoun's antecedent. If a pronoun does not agree with its antecedent, cross the pronoun out and write the correct pronoun above it. The first one has been done for you.

1. Kerry and Sydney first got the idea of clowning from *their* ~~her~~ aunt and uncle.

2. Clown camp included not only local students but also people from many other states, and they lasted all morning every day for one week.

3. Some people returned to camp so they could learn new tricks.

4. The beginning clowns needed to pick their names.

5. Kerry chose *Peppermint* because it is pink and white.

6. Mom made Kerry's costume of pink polka-dotted material, and she sewed a big plastic hoop in the waist.

★ **ELPS** 3E, 4C, 5D, 5E

7. The curly pink wig and costume made Kerry look like a real circus clown when she wore it.

8. Putting on makeup took a long time for Kerry, and I got to help her.

9. Mom told Kerry, "Sydney can draw a big red smile to match your red rubber nose."

10. The goofy shoes and floppy neck ruffle looked perfect; it added pizzazz to the outfit!

The Next Step Write an interesting sentence about something unusual that you have done. Exchange sentences with a partner. Then write a second sentence by replacing one of your partner's nouns with a pronoun. Check for pronoun agreement.

_____

_____

_____

_____

_____

_____

_____

_____

 **ELPS** 2C, 4C, 5D

Pronoun-Antecedent Agreement 2

An **antecedent** is the noun that a pronoun replaces. Each pronoun in your sentences must agree with its antecedent. (See *Texas Write Source* page 445.)

Examples

Mom said, "I want to see Niagara Falls."
(The pronoun *I* and the word it replaces, *Mom*, are singular, so they agree.)

Josh and **Tim** said **they** wanted to go in the tunnel behind the falls.
(The pronoun *they* and the words it replaces, *Josh* and *Tim*, are both plural, so they agree.)

 **Write pronouns in the blanks in the following sentences. Be sure each pronoun agrees with its antecedent. Circle the word or words your pronoun replaces. The first one has been done for you.**

1. (Mom) and (Dad) said ____*they*____ would like to stay on the Canadian side

   of the falls.

2. After Dad checked into the campground, _____ parked the camper.

3. My brothers and I said that _____ wanted to go see the falls.

4. Even before we could see Niagara Falls, we could hear _____.

5. As the wide river spilled over and thundered down, _____

   disappeared in clouds of mist.

6. That night, special lighting cast colors on the mist, making _____

   glow like rainbows in the night!

ELPS 4C, 5D, 5E

7. We needed rain gear to go in the tunnel because _____ was

very wet.

8. My brothers and I looked funny in the thin yellow raincoats _____

had to wear, but Mom and Dad looked even funnier.

9. As we stood at the lookout behind the wall of water, we were glad to

have the raincoats because _____ protected us from the cold mist.

10. Other people were taking boat tours on *The Maid of the Mist* that

carried _____ right into the mist at the base of the falls.

The Next Step Write a paragraph about a special place you have visited. When you finish, circle all the pronouns you have used. See if you can find the antecedent for each one of them. Sometimes an antecedent is in a previous sentence instead of in the same sentence.

_____

_____

_____

_____

_____

_____

_____

Types of Verbs

Review the information about **verbs** on *Texas Write Source* pages 449–450 and 616 before you do this activity.

Examples

Action Verb: Most dogs **chase** cats.

Linking Verb: Our dog **is** a bulldog.

Helping Verb: He **could** chase a big cat.

 **Directions** Read the following sentences and look at the underlined verbs. Decide whether the verbs are action verbs "A," linking verbs "L," or helping verbs "H." Write the correct letter above each verb. The first one has been done for you.

1. Rolf, our bulldog, <u>loves</u> doggy biscuits.

   A (above loves)

2. Those biscuits must <u>taste</u> good, because he <u>hides</u> them everywhere.

3. Then he <u>can</u> <u>snack</u> anytime.

4. I <u>have</u> <u>found</u> biscuits in my shoes.

5. Dad <u>has</u> <u>spotted</u> biscuits under his chewed-up gloves.

6. Rolf <u>chews</u> gloves, too . . . and socks.

7. Oh, yes, and Rolf <u>sneaks</u> cookies, but only the fresh-baked kind.

8. Our family <u>has</u> <u>grown</u> fond of Rolf, though.

9. At least he <u>smells</u> sweet.

10. Rolf always <u>spills</u> my bath powder on his way through the bathroom.

ELPS 4C

ELPS 2C, 2G, 4C

Linking Verbs

A **linking verb** links the subject of a sentence to a noun or an adjective in the predicate. (See *Texas Write Source* page 450 and 616.2.)

Examples

Lunch smells good.
(The verb *smells* links *lunch* to the predicate adjective *good*.)

Our meal is soup.
(The verb *is* links *meal* to the predicate noun *soup*.)

 **Directions** In the following sentences, underline the linking verb and circle the predicate noun or predicate adjective. Draw an arrow from the predicate noun or predicate adjective back to the subject it is linked to. Write "N" to indicate a predicate noun and "A" to indicate a predicate adjective. The first sentence has been done for you.

1. The largest ancient elephant <u>was</u> the imperial woolly (mammoth). *N*

2. The huge tusks were weapons used against predators.

3. Mammoths were the monsters of long ago.

4. An ancient man seems small next to such a beast.

5. The mammoth's hair feels coarse.

6. After thousands of years, frozen mammoths in Siberia still look powerful.

7. Mammoths were food for ancient people.

8. For thousands of years, mammoths have been extinct.

Learning Language Write a sentence for each of the following linking verbs: *is, were, look,* and *appear.* Link two of the subjects to predicate adjectives, and link the other two subjects to predicate nouns. Then read your sentences aloud to a partner. Ask your partner to listen carefully for the predicate nouns and adjectives.

ELPS 2C, 4C, 5D, 5E

Helping Verbs

A **helping verb** comes before the main verb. It helps to describe an action or to show the time of the action. (See *Texas Write Source* page 450 and 616.3.)

Examples

We **could have** cut the tree down.

We **will** move the driveway instead.

Directions In the sentences below, circle each helping verb and underline the verb it helps. The first sentence has been done for you.

1. Shaneesha (was) going to the library.

2. She was working on a book report about *Mississippi Bridge*.

3. I asked her if she would take my books back.

4. She said I should go to the library, too.

5. "Diana might come, too," Shaneesha said, "so we could all work on our book reports."

6. "That would work well, since I am planning to do mine today."

7. "So, I shall see you there?"

8. "I will ask my mom if it's okay," I answered.

9. Shaneesha said, "If she says you may come, meet us where we were sitting last week."

Learning Language Write some sentences that use the words *would, shall,* and *might*. Exchange your work with a partner. Make sure your helping verbs agree.

ELPS 4C, 5E

Directions Underline the verb in each sentence below. Then rewrite each sentence two times, adding a different helping verb each time. (See *Texas Write Source* page 616 for a list of helping verbs.) An example has been done for you.

1. Jamie <u>plays</u> the flute.

   Jamie <u>is</u> playing the flute.

   Jamie <u>will</u> play the flute.

2. Tomás helps his little brother.

   _____

   _____

3. Kerry and Jim walk to school.

   _____

   _____

4. We write stories.

   _____

   _____

5. Carlos rides the bus to work.

   _____

   _____

 **ELPS** 2C, 4C, 5E

Simple Verb Tenses

There are three simple tenses. The **present tense** of a verb states an action that is happening now or that happens regularly. The **past tense** of a verb states an action that happened at a specific time in the past. The **future tense** of a verb states an action that will take place sometime in the future. (See *Texas Write Source* page 451 and 618.1–618.3.)

Examples

Present Tense:
The cricket, mouse, and cat **enjoy** talking to one another.

Past Tense:
They **pranced** about the newsstand half the night.

Future Tense:
These three characters **will win** the hearts of their readers.

 The examples above are about the animals in *The Cricket in Times Square* by George Selden. Now it is your turn to write some sentences about imaginary animals that you have read about or seen in a cartoon. Write at least two sentences for each of the tenses.

Present Tense: _____

_____

_____

Past Tense: _____

_____

_____

Future Tense: _____

_____

ELPS 3E, 4C, 5E

Directions

Write two paragraphs in the space below. First, write about the way something was 50 years ago (food, entertainment, cars). Write this paragraph in the past tense. Next, write a paragraph about the way you think something will be in the future (cars, schools, television). Write this paragraph in the future tense. Share your writing with a classmate.

_____

_____

_____

_____

_____

_____

_____

_____

_____

_____

_____

_____

_____

_____

⭐ **ELPS** 2C, 4C, 5D, 5E

Perfect Tenses 1

The **present perfect tense** states an action that began in the past and is still going on. This tense adds *have* or *has* to the past participle form of the main verb. The **past perfect tense** states an action that began and ended in the past. It adds *had* to the past participle. (See *Texas Write Source* page 452 and 618.4–618.5.)

Examples

Present Perfect: That candle **has burned** for the last 30 hours.

Past Perfect: The forest fire **had burned** out three weeks ago.

Directions ▶ In the sentences that follow, write the correct present perfect or past perfect form of the verb. The first one has been done for you.

has continued
1. The opening act <u>continue</u> for at least 30 minutes. (*present perfect*)

2. The bypass construction <u>take</u> several months to complete. (*past perfect*)

3. Overflowing rivers <u>flood</u> a large part of the county. (*present perfect*)

4. The long journey to the West Coast <u>begin</u>. (*present perfect*)

5. The tree <u>fall</u> more than 60 feet onto the rocks below. (*past perfect*)

6. The run of salmon <u>move</u> quickly upstream. (*present perfect*)

7. By Thursday evening, the men <u>lose</u> the trail. (*past perfect*)

8. With the arrival of the cold north wind, the time <u>came</u> to put on storm windows. (*past perfect*)

9. The flock of geese <u>fly</u> more than 150 miles so far. (*present perfect*)

The Next Step Write about the seasons of the year. Write one sentence using the present perfect tense and one sentence using the past perfect tense.

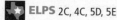 ELPS 2C, 4C, 5D, 5E

Perfect Tenses 2

The **future perfect tense** states an action that will begin in the future and end at a specific time. It adds *will have* to the past participle of the main verb. (See 618.6.)

Example

By next Friday evening, Rayanne will have finished her art project.

 **Directions** In the following sentences, underline the verbs. Label each present perfect tense verb "PR," each past perfect tense verb "PP," and each future perfect tense verb "FP." The first one has been done for you.

PR

1. It's Tuesday, and Chantel <u>has started</u> to hike this trail.

2. She will have hiked more than 50 miles by Thursday afternoon.

3. Chantel and her parents had planned this trip last winter.

4. After her final hike in August, she will have visited five national parks.

5. Chantel's parents have gone with her on each trail.

6. They had bought a weatherproof camera to record their trips.

7. By mid-September, Chantel will have written a report about her adventures.

8. She has begun to arrange all the photos she took along the trails.

9. Chantel had learned about hiking and camping from her parents.

10. By mid-October, she will have presented her report to her class.

The Next Step In three sentences, use the future perfect tense to write about three things you plan to accomplish in the coming months.

 **TEKS** 5.20A(i)
ELPS 3C, 3E, 4C, 4G

Active and Passive Verbs

A verb is **active** if the subject is doing the action. A verb is **passive** if the subject is not doing the action. (See *Texas Write Source* 620.2.)

Examples

Active: The glacier **crushed** the land beneath it.
(The subject *glacier* did the action.)

Passive: The land **was crushed** by the glacier.
(The subject *land* is not doing the action.)

Directions ▶ Underline the verbs. Label them "A" for active or "P" for passive.

1   Glaciers <u>have covered</u> *(A)* much of North America and

2   have melted away several times over thousands of years.

3   Sometimes mountains were cut in half, and V-shaped valleys

4   were turned into U-shaped valleys by these great rivers of ice.

5   Glaciers carried huge boulders hundreds of miles. Today, these

6   large rocks can be seen throughout northern states such as

7   Minnesota and Wisconsin. The Great Lakes were carved out of

8   soft rock, due to the incredible weight of the ice. At the end of

9   each ice age, the glaciers melted and left soil, rocks, and a lot of

10   water behind. Melting glaciers formed ridges of gravel, lakes, and

11   streams. In fact, glaciers changed this continent dramatically.

Learning Language Write several sentences about glaciers, using both active and passive verbs. Then tell a few sentences to a partner. Take notes on what your partner writes and says.

 TEKS 5.20A(i)

> **Directions** ▶ Underline the verbs in each sentence. Label them "A" for active or "P" for passive. The first sentence has been done for you.

              A

1. My sister <u>adores</u> the process of making pottery.

2. This beautiful but delicate vase was made three years ago, when she first began molding clay.

3. The clay was placed in a fiery kiln.

4. The vase was painted with a special glaze to make it waterproof.

5. I prefer to dive into my oil paints and spread them over a canvas.

6. Yellow undertones peek through my painting and give it a bright mood.

7. My teacher gave me a great book about how to use watercolors.

8. The pages are filled with tips about using the paints properly.

> **Directions** ▶ Now rewrite the sentences that had passive verbs. Make them active verbs.

_____

_____

_____

_____

_____

Learning Language Tell a partner about a hobby, such as art or music. Use active verbs.

★ **TEKS** 5.20A(i)
ELPS 2C, 3C, 3E, 4C, 5E

Irregular Verbs 1

Irregular verbs don't play by the rules! When you make them past tense, you can't just add *-ed* as you do with regular verbs. The spelling of irregular verbs changes with different tenses.

Example

Irregular Verbs: catch   caught   caught

Directions ▶ Study the irregular verbs on *Texas Write Source* page 622. Close your book and fill in the missing words on the lines below.

present tense	past tense	past participle
1. blow		*blown*
2. bring		*brought*
3. draw		
4. eat	*ate*	
5. fly		
6. hide	*hid*	
7. know		
8. lay *(to put in place)*		
9. lie *(to recline)*	*lay*	
10. run		*run*

Learning Language Write a few sentences using the words *lay, lie, laid,* and *lain.* Then tell a partner two sentences using other words from your chart.

TEKS 5.20A(i)
ELPS 1B, 1C, 2C, 3C, 3E,
4C, 5E

Irregular Verbs 2

Irregular verbs are not normal! Whenever you change these verbs to past tense or use them with a helping verb, the spelling changes. The only way to know how they change is to learn the different forms of each verb.

Examples

Irregular Verbs: speak   spoke   spoken

fly   flew   flown

 **Directions** Fill in the chart below to see how well you know the different irregular verb forms. The first one has been done for you. When you finish, write three sentences that use different forms of one of these irregular verbs.

Present Tense	Past Tense	Past Participle
see	*saw*	*seen*
	wrote	
drive		
		frozen
	burst	
begin		
		blown
	gave	

Learning Language Use the chart on *Texas Write Source* page 622 to check your work. List any verbs that you got wrong, and tell a partner a sentence for each one.

 **TEKS** 5.20A(i)
ELPS 4C, 5D

Irregular Verbs Review

This activity is a review of some of the **irregular verbs** you have practiced.

 Underline the verb in each sentence below. Then rewrite each sentence two times. The first time, change the verb to past tense. The second time, change the verb to past perfect tense and use the correct past participle form for your main verb. The first sentence has been done for you.

1. Mike <u>brings</u> his turtle to school.

past tense: _____ *Mike <u>brought</u> his turtle to school.* _____

past perfect tense: _____ *Mike <u>had brought</u> his turtle to school.* _____

2. Schuyler eats a box of raisins.

past tense: _____

past perfect tense: _____

3. We see our teacher's car.

past tense: _____

past perfect tense: _____

4. Amber writes a mystery.

past tense: _____

past perfect tense: _____

5. Our neighbor gives us tomatoes.

past tense: _____

past perfect tense: _____

 **ELPS** 2C, 4C, 5G

Proper and Common Adjectives

An **adjective** describes a noun or a pronoun. Adjectives can be common or proper. A **proper adjective** is capitalized and often tells the origin.

Examples

The dog has long ears. The German shepherd chewed on a bone.

 **Directions** Write a paragraph that compares and contrasts the three dogs below. Include at least three common adjectives and a proper adjective in your paragraph. Circle the adjectives and share your paragraph with a partner.

_____

_____

_____

_____

Learning Language Imagine you have a dog named Ralph. Write a name poem using common and proper adjectives to describe him. Then tell a partner a sentence using an adjective.

R _____

A _____

L _____

P _____

H _____

ELPS 3C, 3E, 4C, 5G

Directions In the following paragraph, label the adjectives. Write "C" above common adjectives and "P" above proper adjectives. The first one has been done for you. (Note: "Rocky Mountains," "grizzly bears," and "mountain lions" are nouns.)

P

1 The Colorado Rocky Mountains have a breathtaking

2 appearance that seems almost unreal. The jagged peaks look

3 like the Swiss Alps and cut through gray, hovering clouds. The

4 snow-covered mountainsides reflect blinding sunshine similar to

5 what you would see over the hot Sahara sand of the desert. The

6 massive formations serve as a wilderness home to golden-brown

7 grizzly bears, sleek mountain lions, and towering, long-legged

8 moose.

Learning Language Below are some adjectives that give only a vague picture of what is being described. After each adjective, write three other adjectives that have similar meanings but are more colorful. Use a thesaurus if you need to. An example has been done for you.

1. large ___*gigantic*___ ___*tremendous*___ ___*extensive*___

2. small _____ _____ _____

3. loud _____ _____ _____

4. old _____ _____ _____

5. nice _____ _____ _____

6. fun _____ _____ _____

Tell a partner a sentence using one of your new adjectives.

⭐ **ELPS** 2C, 4C

Predicate Adjectives

A **predicate adjective** follows a linking verb and describes the subject. (See *Texas Write Source* 624.3.)

Examples

The fish were luminous in the undersea sunlight.

Our snorkeling adventure became scary when we spotted the barracuda.

> **Directions** ▶ In the following paragraph, replace each underlined predicate adjective with a more colorful adjective. The first one has been done for you.

thrilling

1 Our family's Florida vacation was ~~fun~~. The plane we flew on was

2 big. When I looked out the windows, cars and trucks looked small

3 from thousands of feet up in the air. Buildings and fields were big, like

4 huge patchwork quilts. Roads were long and made odd patterns. Tall,

5 puffy clouds were big, like white mountains right outside our window.

6 Some were fine mist. Others were big, like moving marshmallows.

7 When the sunlight hit a river just right, the light appeared bright, like

8 a camera flash. The speed of the plane became slow, and we spotted

9 the runway and some palm trees. The captain's voice was loud as he

10 announced that we would soon be landing.

★ ELPS 2C, 4C

Indefinite Adjectives

Indefinite adjectives describe approximate amounts of "how much" and "how many." These amounts are estimates rather than exact counts. (See *Texas Write Source* 626.1.)

Examples

There were **many** people at the car races.

Some rain fell during the day.

 **Directions** ▶ Write a sentence for each of the following words. Use the word as an adjective. The first one has been done for you.

1. few *Our teacher says few people study the ocean's volcanoes.*

   _____

2. many _____

   _____

3. most _____

   _____

4. some _____

   _____

5. all _____

   _____

6. several _____

   _____

TEKS 5.20A(iii)
ELPS 2C, 4C

Forms of Adjectives

The **comparative** form of an adjective compares two things. It is formed by adding -*er* to a one-syllable adjective and *more* or *less* before a longer adjective. The **superlative** form of an adjective compares three or more things. It is formed by adding -*est* to a one-syllable adjective and *most* or *least* to a longer adjective. Also read about **irregular forms** at 626.5.

Examples

Positive:	Comparative:	Superlative:
smart	smarter	smartest
glorious	more glorious	most glorious

Directions Fill in each blank with the correct form of the underlined adjective. The first one has been done for you.

1. Todd's dog is <u>big</u>, but Samantha's dog is _____*bigger*_____, and

   Charlotte's dog is the _____*biggest*_____ dog I've ever seen.

2. Danielle has <u>many</u> relatives, but Paulo has _____, and Chet

   has the _____ relatives of us all.

3. Katie is <u>funny</u>, but Marsha is even _____, and Emily is the

   _____ of all the girls in our class.

4. Vanilla ice cream is <u>good</u>, but chocolate is _____, and

   chocolate chocolate-chip ice cream is the _____ of all.

5. Summer is a <u>beautiful</u> time of year, but fall is _____, and

   spring is the _____ of all the seasons.

⭐ **TEKS** 5.20A(iii)
ELPS 2G, 3C, 3E, 4C

Directions ▶ **Read the following sentences and then fill in each blank with the correct form of the adjective shown in parentheses. The first one has been done for you.**

1. Shoes come in ___*many*___ sizes and shapes. *(many)*

2. Though shoes are made from many materials, the _____ ones are made of leather. *(good)*

3. Canvas tennis shoes are _____ than leather tennis shoes. *(cheap)*

4. Synthetic materials make modern hiking shoes _____ than those of the past. *(light)*

5. Even inexpensive hiking shoes are _____. *(tough)*

6. Steel-toed work boots are _____ than regular boots. *(safe)*

7. After leaving Shoe Mart, Maggie discovered a shoe store at the mall with _____ shoes at reduced prices. *(many)*

8. Men's shoes are often _____ than women's shoes. *(large)*

9. Mom's sandals are her _____ footwear. *(comfortable)*

10. Young children think shoes with flashing colored lights are the _____ shoes they could ever have. *(pretty)*

11. Slip-on shoes are _____ for children to put on than tie shoes. *(easy)*

12. Shoes with a steel shank in the sole are _____ than shoes without that support. *(strong)*

Learning Language Tell a partner two sentences. Use *stronger* in one sentence, and use *strongest* in the other. Then listen to make sure your partner does the same correctly.

TEKS 5.20A(iv)
ELPS 2C, 4C

Types of Adverbs

There are four basic types of **adverbs**: adverbs of *place*, *manner*, *time*, and *degree*. Adverbs describe a verb, an adjective, or another adverb. (See *Texas Write Source* pages 460 and 628.)

Examples

Place: The car swerved left to miss a hole.

Manner: The driver mumbled loudly.

Time: He would complain to the city later.

Degree: For now he was totally relieved.

Directions In each of the following sentences, circle the adverb and draw an arrow to the word it describes. On the line after the sentence, write whether the adverb is one of "place," "manner," "time," or "degree." The first sentence has been done for you. When you finish, say one of the adverbs you circled in a sentence.

1. Jody and I (often) go to the park.   *time*

2. Sometimes we play softball.   _____

3. We choose our teams carefully.   _____

4. We play hard.   _____

5. Jody and I always pitch.   _____

6. Tasha barely caught the pop fly.   _____

7. Ira hits the ball hard.   _____

8. Most fielders step back for Ira.   _____

9. Monica easily catches ground balls.   _____

10. Tyrone completely missed first base.   _____

182

 TEKS 5.20A(iv)
ELPS 1E, 3C, 3F, 4C

 **Directions** In each of the following sentences, add an adverb of the type in parentheses. Write the new sentence on the line. Then circle the adverb and draw a line to the word it describes. The first one has been done for you.

1. I'm going to the park. *(time)*   *I'm going to the park later.*

2. Marcia eats. *(manner)* _____

3. Rodrigo laughs. *(manner)* _____

4. Let's go swimming. *(time)* _____

5. Let's go for a walk. *(place)* _____

6. Arlene noticed a robin. *(degree)* _____

Learning Language Write a personal narrative paragraph about your favorite game, sport, or pastime. Use adverbs to tell about time, place, manner, and degree. Underline all of your adverbs. Then share your paragraph with a partner. Ask your partner to circle two adverbs and use them in a sentence.

_____
_____
_____
_____
_____
_____
_____

TEKS 5.20A(iv)
ELPS 3C, 3E, 4C

Forms of Adverbs

Review *Texas Write Source* pages 460 and 630. Then complete this activity using the **comparative** and **superlative** forms of adverbs.

Examples

Positive:	Comparative:	Superlative:
near	nearer	nearest
softly	more softly	most softly

 **Directions** Rewrite each sentence twice. Use the comparative form in the first sentence and the superlative form in the second sentence. When you finish, tell a partner three sentences using different forms of the word *quietly*.

1. Gabriella runs <u>fast</u>.

Gabriella runs <u>faster</u> than Sarah.

Teri runs <u>fastest</u> of all.

2. Bruce played <u>well</u>.

_____

_____

3. Larissa plays her CD's <u>loudly</u>.

_____

_____

4. Terrence reads <u>slowly</u>.

_____

_____

 **TEKS** 5.20A(iv)
ELPS 3C, 3E, 4C

Directions **Think of three adverbs that describe how something is done. Then write sentences using the positive, comparative, and superlative forms of each adverb. One has been done for you.**

1. adverb = *carefully*

   Jim writes his stories <u>carefully</u>.

   Rosa writes hers <u>more carefully</u> than Jim writes his.

   Clare writes hers the <u>most carefully</u> of all.

2. adverb = _____

   _____

   _____

   _____

3. adverb = _____

   _____

   _____

   _____

4. adverb = _____

   _____

   _____

   _____

Learning Language **Tell a partner three sentences using the following adverbs correctly:** *easily, more easily, most easily.*

★ **TEKS** 5.20A(v)
ELPS 2C, 4C

Prepositional Phrases 1

Prepositional phrases include a preposition, the object of the preposition, and any words that modify the object. A prepositional phrase doesn't have a subject or a predicate. However, it can provide details or add important information about location, time, or direction.

Example

(preposition)

We have an aquarium in our classroom.

(prepositional phrase)

Directions ▶ Circle each preposition and underline each prepositional phrase.

1. Patches ran (around) the room and then jumped (onto) the table.

2. Tom is in his room, hiding under his bed.

3. We went to a restaurant before the play.

4. This book was written by my favorite author.

5. After lunch, we have free time until 1:00.

6. My paper is under that pile of books on the desk.

7. Becky left her skates outside the door and went into the house.

8. She walked through the kitchen toward the stairs.

9. My house is near the corner of Fifth Street and Central Avenue.

10. Go past two stop signs and turn right at Fifth Street.

★ **TEKS** 5.20A(v)
ELPS 4C, 5G

 Replace the underlined preposition so the new prepositional phrase means the opposite. The first one has been done for you.

from

1. Frank is walking <u>to</u> the barn.

2. Marie is sitting <u>inside</u> the car.

3. Blaine hit the ball <u>under</u> the fence.

4. After checking the map for the third time, Bill walked <u>down</u> the steps.

5. Elaine spotted a deer <u>in front of</u> the tree.

6. Rafe's little brother jumped <u>on</u> the green couch.

7. <u>After</u> the game, we ate brats, potato chips, and ice cream.

8. Hanna went to the craft fair <u>without</u> her friends.

9. Lane got his lunch and sat down at the table <u>across from</u> Jorge.

10. Janelle walked <u>through</u> the deep mud puddle.

11. Ready for the next task, Gere walked <u>out of</u> the gym.

Learning Language Write three sentences about a weekend activity, using prepositional phrases in the sentences. Then have a partner tell you each sentence with the preposition changed to mean the opposite.

_____

_____

_____

_____

★ **TEKS** 5.20A(v)
ELPS 4C

Prepositional Phrases 2

Turn to *Texas Write Source* pages 462 and 632 for more information about **prepositions** and **prepositional phrases**.

Example

(preposition)

The stream flowed out of Bridge Lake.

(prepositional phrase)

Directions ▶ In the sentences below, write an appropriate preposition in each blank provided and then underline the prepositional phrase. The first one has been done for you. Then pick one of the adjectives and say it in a sentence.

1   Each summer, my brother Steven and I looked forward to floating

2   _____*down*_____ the stream _____ our grandfather's

3   cabin. We each slipped big black inner tubes _____ our

4   heads and jumped _____ the dock. First, we ducked

5   down as we went _____ the wooden bridge. Then we

6   stayed close together as we paddled _____ the cattails

7   and weeds _____ the meandering stream. I liked to

8   have my brother _____ the lead. Once he shouted when

9   he saw a water snake swimming _____ us. Usually,

10   _____ the clear water, we watched the schools

TEKS 5.20A(v)
ELPS 2E, 2I, 3B, 3E, 4C

11 _____ minnows swimming _____ us.

12 _____ many bends and some shallow spots, we finally

13 came _____ our favorite spot—a big culvert going

14 _____ a road. Our yells echoed as we shot through

15 _____ the other side. Then we swirled _____

16 a churning circle _____ a big, gentle whirlpool.

Learning Language Write a sentence for each of the prepositional phrases below. Illustrate your favorite sentence. Then tell your sentence to a partner and show your picture. Summarize what you see in your partner's picture.

1. in the house

_____

_____

2. behind the house

_____

_____

3. throughout the house

_____

_____

4. for the house

_____

_____

ELPS 1C, 2C, 4C, 5F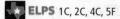

Coordinating Conjunctions

Coordinating conjunctions connect equal parts. For example, coordinating conjunctions can connect two words, two phrases, or two clauses. (See *Texas Write Source* pages 463 and 634.)

Example

My cookie jar is full, **but** it is full of dog biscuits.

Directions | **Read and memorize the coordinating conjunctions below. Use these conjunctions to fill in the blanks in the sentences.**

and	but	or	so	yet

1. My dog Harold is small _____ strong.

2. He has white paws _____ shaggy ears.

3. All afternoon he sleeps on the porch _____ in the house.

4. When I get home, he wants to run _____ play.

5. Harold is fat _____ fast.

6. He chases squirrels _____ our cat.

7. Harold is seven years old _____ still plays like a puppy.

8. He growls at other dogs _____ hides during storms.

9. Harold likes to swim in the lake, _____ he doesn't like being out in the rain.

★ **TEKS** 5.21B(i)
ELPS 4C, 5F

 **Directions** ▶ Use a comma plus a coordinating conjunction from the list on page 189 to connect each pair of simple sentences below.

1. Harold loves dog food. He loves people food, too.

   _____

   _____

2. I give Harold cookies. He's always happy to see me.

   _____

   _____

3. He likes hamburgers. He's not supposed to have them.

   _____

   _____

4. Harold loves bones. He looks for them in grocery bags.

   _____

   _____

5. Harold likes to swim in the lake. He chases the Canada geese.

   _____

   _____

6. Harold barks at our cat. He never barks at strangers.

   _____

   _____

TEKS 5.20A(vii)
ELPS 1C, 2C, 4C, 5F

Subordinating Conjunctions

Use a **subordinating conjunction** to connect two clauses to make a complex sentence. A dependent clause often begins with a subordinating conjunction such as *because* or *since*.

Example

We didn't have time to go fishing although we had poles and bait.

 **Directions**
Choose subordinating conjunctions from the list and write them on the lines to complete the story.

> after, although, as, because, before, if, in order that, since, so, that, though, unless, until, when, where, while

1 We were in art class _____ our principal reminded

2 us that the dress rehearsal for the concert would begin at 6:00 p.m.

3 sharp! _____ Matt missed the rehearsal and arrived

4 just before the concert, the choir director told Matt _____

5 he would have to miss out on the party. _____ the

6 concert was over, Matt disappeared. We spotted him using the office

7 phone. Later, we were surprised to see that Matt was allowed to be at

8 the party _____ we heard his reason for being late. His

9 new brother had just been born! _____ Matt knew he had

10 a new brother, he wasn't sure what the baby had been named.

192

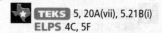 TEKS 5, 20A(vii), 5.21B(i)
ELPS 4C, 5F

 **In the exercise below, combine each pair of clauses to form a complex sentence using the subordinating conjunction shown in parentheses. Remember to use correct punctuation and capitalization. The first one has been done for you.**

1. the day was sunny   the air was very cold   *(although)*

   Although the day was sunny, the air was very cold.

2. the food was cooked   everyone was served   *(after)*

   _____

3. everyone was surprised   Bob ran into the room   *(when)*

   _____

4. Jamie held the form   Lana filled it with plaster   *(while)*

   _____

5. a part was missing   James couldn't finish the model   *(because)*

   _____

6. Laz didn't have enough trouble   his bike pedal broke   *(as if)*

   _____

7. the bell rang   students could not leave the building   *(until)*

   _____

8. Penny bought the hat   the sale ended   *(before)*

   _____

Learning Language Using *after, when, though,* and *because,* tell a partner several complex sentences about a game you have played with friends.

TEKS 5.20A(viii)
ELPS 2C, 4C

Transitional Words

Transitional words connect ideas and show how the ideas are related. They can help you organize your writing. (See *Texas Write Source* pages 490 and 491.)

Example

First, Tommy cracked two eggs in a bowl.
Then, he whisked them together.

Directions **Fill in the blanks in the paragraph about the book, *Where the Red Fern Grows*. Use transitional words from the list. The first one has been done for you.**

finally	first	next	after	then	also

When Billy decided he wanted two redbone hounds, nothing

could stop him. _____*First*_____, he found an advertisement

that said how much the pups would cost. _____, he

cleaned up an old K.C. Baking Powder can and used it as a bank.

_____, he worked hard for two years to save enough

money for his pups. He picked berries, sold bait to the fishermen, and

worked in his grandfather's store. He _____ did many

odd jobs to earn money. _____ two years, Billy had

enough money. He raced triumphantly to his grandfather's store and

gave him the money for the pups. _____, Billy became

the proud owner of two hound pups: Old Dan and Little Ann.

TEKS 5.20A(viii)
ELPS 4C, 5F

Directions Fill in the blanks using the following transitional words.

as a result	instead of	first	then

_____, Tony went to the store to buy a loaf

of bread. _____, he went to the park to play ball.

_____ going directly home, Tony decided to go to the

river to feed the ducks some bread. _____, Tony got

home late and only had a half of the loaf left to eat.

Directions Write a paragraph that persuades someone to think differently. Use and underline the following transitional words: *in addition, for example, therefore, most importantly.*

_____

_____

_____

_____

_____

_____

_____

Learning Language Tell a partner three sentences that summarize the paragraph you just wrote. Remember to use transitional words.

ELPS 4C

Conjunctions Review

This activity is a review of coordinating and subordinating **conjunctions**. (See *Texas Write Source* pages 463 and 634.1–634.2.)

Directions ▶ **Each of the sentences below has one coordinating conjunction and one subordinating conjunction. Underline both, and write "C" above each coordinating conjunction and "S" above each subordinating conjunction. The first sentence has been done for you.**

1. Let's shoot baskets <u>or</u> play catch <u>until</u> it gets dark.
       C   *S*

2. While it is snowing, we can make a snowman and a snow fort.

3. The new boy doesn't know us, but he'll come to our party if we invite him.

4. My mom and I like to watch videos when it's rainy.

5. When our teacher is sick, Mr. Diaz or another substitute comes to our class.

6. Tina does her homework and her chores before she eats dinner.

7. We heard the kitten mewing, yet we couldn't tell if the sound was coming from the closet.

8. Juan and I walked home after we watched the fireworks.

9. Terri wants to come over, but she can't come unless she gets over her cold.

10. Because it is snowing, school may be canceled or delayed.

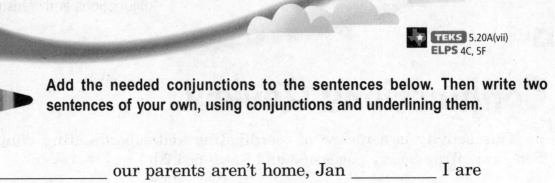

TEKS 5.20A(vii)
ELPS 4C, 5F

Directions Add the needed conjunctions to the sentences below. Then write two sentences of your own, using conjunctions and underlining them.

1. _____ our parents aren't home, Jan _____ I are

   making dinner.

2. Jared _____ my sister walks the dog _____ we leave for

   school.

3. It's Monday, _____ there is no school _____ it's a

   holiday.

4. _____ the thunderstorm, the sun came out, _____ the

   air was still cold, _____ it was windy.

5. _____

   _____

   _____

6. _____

   _____

   _____

Learning Language Tell a partner two sentences. Use *unless* in the first sentence. Use *so* in the second sentence.

★ **ELPS** 2C, 4C, 5F

Interjections

An **interjection** is a word or phrase used to express a strong emotion or surprise. A comma or an exclamation point is used to separate an interjection from the rest of the sentence. (See *Texas Write Source* page 636.)

Examples

Holy cow! That ball is out of here!

Oh, there it is.

Directions ▶ Pretend you have just spent some time with a herpetologist (someone who works with snakes and other reptiles). Write a postcard telling a friend how you felt about being around snakes. Use interjections to let your friend know how strongly you felt about the experience.

_____ , 20 ___

Dear _____ ,

_____   _____

_____   _____

_____

_____

Your friend,

_____

TEKS 5.20A(ii–vii)
ELPS 1E, 3E, 4C, 5F

Parts of Speech Review 1

Directions Write the part of speech for each list of words on the line in the circle. See *Texas Write Source* page 636 for a list of the eight parts of speech.

piggy bank
money
class
wallet
_____

spend
saved
count
give
_____

we
they
anybody
ours
_____

selfishly
really
usually
very
_____

wealthy
cheapest
generous
more
_____

in
with
out of
while
_____

Wow!
Yes!
Hey!
Eureka!
_____

and
but
or
because
_____

Learning Language Now write a sentence using as many of the parts of speech as you can. Use some of the words in the circles. Tell another sentence to a partner. Have your partner identify three of the words you used and name their part of speech.

TEKS 5.20A(iv), 5.20A(v), 5.20A(vii)
ELPS 2G, 3E, 4C

Parts of Speech Review 2

This activity is a review of all the **parts of speech** you have studied.

Directions ▶ Below is a fable from Aesop. Above each underlined word, write what part of speech the word is. The first two have been done for you.

The Crow and the Pitcher

                          noun   *verb*
1   Once there was a <u>crow</u> who was so thirsty he couldn't <u>speak</u>. He

2   found a <u>large</u> pitcher of water <u>in</u> a garden. He <u>lowered</u> his beak into the

3   pitcher to drink. <u>But</u> there was only a little <u>water</u> in the pitcher, and

4   he couldn't reach it. <u>He</u> thought of breaking the pitcher, but <u>it</u> was too

5   strong. He tried <u>hard</u> to turn the pitcher over, but it was too heavy. The

6   <u>poor</u> crow was about to give up <u>when</u> he <u>noticed</u> some pebbles in the

7   garden. This gave him a wonderful idea. "<u>Yes</u>!" he thought to himself.

8   "I will have a drink after all!" He <u>quickly</u> picked up a pebble in his

9   <u>beak</u> and dropped it <u>into</u> the pitcher. As he did this again <u>and</u> again,

10 the water rose <u>higher</u> and higher in the pitcher. Finally, the crow was

11 able to reach the water and drink.

Learning Language Talk with a partner about how smart the crow is. Use as many parts of speech as you can. Use some of the words from the fable.

ELPS 4C

Parts of Speech Review 3

Directions Read the following paragraph. Then fill in the blanks with examples of nouns, verbs, pronouns, and so on, from the paragraph.

I spotted an old picture of a suburb of Milwaukee, Wisconsin. In black and white, this 100-year-old picture showed very tall trees instead of the huge electrical towers that are there today. The trees appeared to be pine trees, but maybe they were cedars. A dirt path that was only about three feet wide stood in place of busy four-lane roads. Wow! For me, it's rather sad to see a quiet, rural area grow slowly into a small city.

Nouns	Verbs	Pronouns
_____	_____	_____
_____	_____	_____
_____	_____	_____
_____	_____	_____

Adverbs	Adjectives	Prepositions
_____	_____	_____
_____	_____	_____
_____	_____	_____
_____	_____	_____

Interjections	Conjunctions
_____	_____
	_____

TEKS 5.15D
ELPS 1E

Editing Review 1

In this activity, you will practice correcting different kinds of grammatical errors.

Directions ▶ Read the following story. Label the underlined words "C" for correct, or cross out the words and correct the grammatical error. The first one has been done for you.

1   Keisha wanted Amanda and ~~I~~ *me* to go to the movies. We

2   <u>bought</u> a few snacks and drinks and then went to <u>chose</u> a seat.

3   Keisha didn't want <u>no</u> aisle seat, and Amanda refused to sit in

4   the middle. During the movie, Keisha <u>couldn't hardly</u> quit talking.

5   I asked her nicely to be quiet, but <u>her</u> got offended.

6   The movie <u>wasn't</u> all that great. The plot was horrible and

7   the actors <u>was</u> awful, too. Most of our friends <u>has seen</u> this movie

8   and liked it. However, I thought it was the <u>most worst</u> movie I

9   ever saw. All of the scenes <u>are</u> filmed underwater, so it was very

10 <u>darker.</u> Halfway through the movie, Keisha and Amanda <u>jumps</u>

11 up and <u>leave</u> me sitting all alone! I <u>runs</u> out to find out what

12 happened. Neither <u>were</u> happy about the movie, so they wanted

13 to leave. Keisha and Amanda <u>is</u> my <u>best</u> friends, but they can be

14 moody. I don't think I'll go with <u>them</u> to the movies <u>no more</u>.

★ TEKS 5.15D
ELPS 1E

Editing Review 2

This activity is a review of some of the grammar skills you have studied.

 **Read the following sentences. Correct the grammatical errors. You may add words or phrases, delete unnecessary words, or change words as needed.**

1. Organized a car wash to raise money for families in need.

_____

_____

2. Sherry and Justin drawed a few signs for the event.

_____

_____

3. The sun was shining in the morning, but in the afternoon.

_____

_____

4. Lightning in the sky, so we ran toward the shelter.

_____

_____

5. We have been soaked, but at least we didn't have to rinse the cars!

_____

_____

Learning Language Tell a partner two sentences about a school fund-raiser. Make sure your sentences do not contain grammatical errors.